9/15/20

To Albany Public Library

Son of Prince Edward County

by Twitty J. Styles, Ph.D.

DORRANCE
PUBLISHING CO
EST. 1920
PITTSBURGH PENNSYLVANIA 15238

Dorrance Publishing Co
585 Alpha Drive
Pittsburgh, PA 15238
Visit our website at *www.dorrancebookstore.com*

ISBN: 978-1-4809-9991-6
eISBN: 978-1-4809-9962-6

PREFACE

Big Man from Farmville

May 18th, 1927 was a grand day for Five Forks, Virginia.
 A midwife brought to light a special being named Winfield,
But this Styles-clan son was soon renamed Twitty with many a
Social glory to settle on his shoulders and emblazon his shield.

The Robert Russa Moton School, ten miles in Farmville,
Was his growing place for eleven years; three prime years
In the classroom of mathematics teacher Dorothy Vaughan still
Teaching us, in *Hidden Figures,* with her team of black peers.

The Moton School is now a historic landmark, an event led
By the courage of Barbara Rose Johns and others in desegregating
Virginia's schools in Davis v. County School Board of Prince Edward
County[1] Lawyers Robinson and Hill acting, May 23rd, 1951; the beginning.

---

[1] *Davis v County School Board of Prince Edward County* (1952) was one of the five cases combined into *Brown v Board of Education* (1954), the famous case in which the U.S. Supreme Court declared that state laws establishing separate public schools for black and white students to be unconstitutional.

After much ado, the U.S. Supreme Court ruled in 1954 toward unity
But the leaders of Prince Edward Schools denied financial support
And some 400 children, until 1964, lost their educational opportunity
Until an order of great power and authority came from a federal court.

The black members of Farmville have purchased the Moton School
From the town for $300,000, and it now celebrates as a museum,
But with little financial contribution from the civic leaders who rule
The state and Prince Edward County, a flaw, wrong, and too sadly seen.

But Robert Russa Moton School was not alone in its backward ways.
Farmville State Teachers College (now Longwood University) also was ill:
Twitty could carry bags for the women of the school, but other forays
Were prohibited. Times have changed and Longwood University as well.

For its anniversary, Union College sent Professor Twitty Styles,
With great pride, as its representative in the doctoral gown of NYU.[2]
This Five Forks man appeared with grace and his radiant smiles
To observe and endorse the people and the schools now truly due.

Constance Glasgow joined Twitty in 1962 from Downstate University
And Auria and Scott with their Jessica and Steven now bloom
In the sacred garden that Stylesian leadership has created for diversity.
Their crucial planting extended to Union College, now with room

For blacks, women and others to build a learning community for unity,
The founding in 1997 of UNITAS, a potent agent for the holy blending
Of this wondrous array of people and places toward one humanity.

---

[2] NYU: New York University

My wife Dena Abigail Wood helped greatly in this needed flowering.

With a gracious and relentless energy, intolerant of the namby-pamby,
Bearer of high standards, master of giving back, patron of arts,
Korean War veteran serving in Japan, wearer of neck-ties quite dandy,
Inspiring chair of Union's Biology Department with administrative smarts,

Twitty, my beloved elder brother for 40 years. I could go on for hours
But in expediency I close, still not fully covering his many powers.

Carl J. George

May 27th, 2017

In celebration of the 90th birthday of Professor Twitty J. Styles, Ph.D.,
with guidance from Dr. Constance Glasgow, M.D., and Commissioner
Osbourne McKay.

CONTENTS

FOREWORD

Many books, newspaper accounts, and treatises have been written about the closing of Robert Russa Moton High School in Farmville, Virginia, and other schools in rural Prince Edward County in the late 1950s. Nationally known reporters from reputable newspapers and mass media outlets have chronicled and filed accounts of their research. Very few of them, if any at all, grew up in Prince Edward County and attended a segregated and unequal school. This is the testimony of Twitty J. Styles, Ph.D., a witness to the flames that burned for years prior to the infamous student-led strike that took place in Farmville in the spring of 1951. At that time, the eyes of the world were focused on both Prince Edward County (PEC) and Farmville, Virginia.

Why is this book so critical and a must read? It chronicles the life of Twitty J. Styles, who was born in Prince Edward County, Virginia, over 90 years ago, and tells the story of how he endured and overcame the oppressive racial segregation practices that began for him in Farmville, Virginia, at the Moton School, which eventually became a test case in the *Brown v Board of Education* (1954) decision that eventually desegregated public schools in America. It also shows how his determination and persistence in having been raised in a single parent home in rural Virginia led him to become a prominent name in higher education in the field of biological sciences, having traveled, taught, and connected with students, faculty, and cultures from all over the world.

Throughout many challenges and obstacles, Twitty evolved into a highly respected man not only for his intellectual prowess but also for being a demanding and caring professor, a man dedicated and committed to improving life for all mankind. He is active in his church, Alpha Phi Alpha Fraternity, Sigma Pi Phi Fraternity (The Boulé), the Rotary Club, and the local Veterans of Foreign Wars Post 1498, to name only a few of the many organizations and boards on which he has served.

Times were challenging for him in the 1930s through the 1960s and, in some instances, even today. Following his discharge from military service, he spent ten years pursuing a doctoral degree in biology at New York University (NYU). The G.I. Bill provided him with money for tuition and books, but he had to work full-time to earn his degree. As he wrote this autobiography, many times he became choked up with emotion as he recalled the trials and tribulations he faced. Following his life-changing experiences in the U.S. Army and earning his Ph.D., the next phase of his life consisted of spending thirty-two years on the faculty of Union College, a private, highly-selective, co-educational college in Schenectady, New York.

His training fortified him to go into the classroom and share with his students what he learned in the Army, at Virginia Union University, and at NYU. From 1950 until 1963, he was away from Farmville and Robert R. Moton H.S., unable to intervene to help his friends, relatives, and the school children deal with the turmoil and strife that so profoundly affected their lives. Today, he is still in touch with some of the leaders of the strike, and together, they reminisce about those difficult and transformative times.

Professor Styles is known for his expertise in parasitology and related subjects. He served as the chairman of the Union College Department of Biological Sciences from 1993-1996 and was the first African American professor to earn tenure in the biology department at Union College (and the second African American professor to earn tenure in any department at Union). He has earned many awards including The Capital District Lifetime Achievement Award (2012), the Jesse Ball Du Pont Fellowship (1991), the Capital District National Pan Hellenic Award, the Meritorious Service Award at Union College (1991), the New York State Senate Korean Veterans Award, and four medals earned for his military service during the Korean War.

ACKNOWLEDGEMENTS

Writing this book has given me the opportunity to tell how the many experiences I have had in my life had their genesis in Five Forks, Virginia, and influenced my development as a husband, father, brother, student, soldier, teacher, and man of color living in a color-restricted society. I have done my best to navigate the discrimination, polarization, segregation, and racial disparity that has not been an insignificant part of my life's journey.

When I started writing this memoir, I thought that it would be hard to recall some of my life's experiences, but as it turned out, my ability to recall them was outstanding. Stored away in the recesses of my mind were experiences that seemed like they had happened just yesterday. I'm thankful that my memory allowed me to relive many of the peaks, valleys, sorrows, and joys I have experienced during my life, and the only regret I have is that there are so many other things that I could not include in this volume. Maybe I'll save them for another edition!

This book is dedicated to my late father, Peter Styles, a proud man who was born humble but realized the value of getting a good education. Although he only finished fourth grade, he had a keen intellect and an inquisitive mind grounded in common sense. He was loving, stern, caring, and sharing of all his energy to make his family better people and citizens. His children were his jewels, pride, and joy, and he successfully raised eight of them as a single parent in racist Virginia during The Great Depression. The legacy of caring and sharing that he so richly bestowed upon me and my siblings has now with the help of my wife, Connie, been passed on to our children Scott, Auria, daughter-in-law Jessica, and grandson Steven.

I sincerely appreciate all the support I have received from family, friends, colleagues, and students who encouraged me to write about my life story, and I'd like to take a few lines to thank the following people in particular: Dr. James Catalfamo, a former student, colleague, and now friend of mine who spent countless hours reading the manuscript and selecting the appropriate pictures for this book. He also worked tirelessly and unselfishly with the publishers to bring this book to fruition. Without him, this book would not have been completed. My son, Mr. Scott Peterson Styles, deserves special recognition for talking with me about my story and spending countless hours reading the final manuscript and making grammatical, stylistic, and syntactic changes to improve the readability and flow of the book. My niece, Ms. Kathy Styles, deserves special recognition for her hard work during the early stages of the manuscript, particularly for countless hours spent typing, editing, and forming the table of contents for this book. Dr. Barbara Lang, also a former student, colleague and now friend deserves special recognition for editing all portions of the book, keeping my spirits up, and making many helpful suggestions. Dr. Frank Romagosa, family friend, professional anthropologist, and business consultant also deserves special recognition for doing the same and also bringing a humanities perspective to the book that sometimes we scientists take for granted. And, last, but not least, I'd also like to thank Mr. Wim Platteborze, our long-time family friend from Belgium and professional graphic artist. He designed the cover of the book and chose its picture.

Once again, I'd like to thank all of the above and my entire immediate and extended family in America and from around the world for your love, friendship, and support in helping me share my story with others. You have no idea how much I truly cherish you all.

INTRODUCTION

In the spirit of friendship and a sense of humor, I hope to leave behind an indelible memory not in stone or mortar but in the minds and hearts of those who knew me. In addition, I hope that readers will understand how Prince Edward County, Virginia, left an everlasting imprint on my life socially, emotionally, and psychologically.

This is a story of a black boy who grew up in Prince Edward County, Virginia, during the Great Depression and attended separate and unequal schools long before *Brown v. Board of Education*. This was the era of Jim Crow, the racial caste system in which blacks could not eat in the same eating establishments or use the same restrooms as whites. Moreover, blacks endured the humiliation of signs that said, "For Coloreds Only," requiring us to sit in the back of busses, trains, and airplanes, and to drink from separate water fountains. As a young child who was taught to think about others in a colorless manner, and who felt he was free, this life was confusing and ugly.

I hope that this book may serve as an inspiration for the "now" generation who I believe should understand that the life they now enjoy has not always been this way. Life for those of us from Prince Edward County, Virginia, was indeed a struggle as we sought to overcome the racial injustices of the Jim Crow era. If but a single reader is made aware of the common values that bind us all as humans, and that obviate the need for racial discord, I will have achieved my goal.

FAMILY REUNION

STYLES FAMILY REUNION
FIVE FORKS, VIRGINIA
AUGUST 5-7, 2016

As we opened the front door of our home in New York State to load our luggage into the car, I noticed it was a beautiful day. The sun was shining, the sky was clear, the birds were chirping in the trees—all signs of a great day ahead. I had a flashback to when I was a child, and my father would come outside for the first time to sit on the porch. If it was a day like today, he would say in a loud and boisterous manner, "Great day in the morning!" with a broad smile.

After loading up the car, Connie and I left home for the Albany County International Airport in Latham, New York. It was a day before the Styles Family Reunion, and we planned to make a stop at Virginia Union University (VUU) in Richmond, Virginia. I wanted to inquire about the Twitty J. Styles Family Endowed Scholarship, which I established in 2013. After the plane took off, we arrived in Philadelphia about ninety minutes later. We had an hour layover before boarding our plane to Richmond. Shortly after boarding the plane, the captain announced, "There is a mechanical problem, and we hope we can fix it in 15 minutes." After hearing this news, I thought I would have a panic attack because it was warm inside, and it was a little hard to breathe. Finally, after about an hour, we took off, and the plane landed in Richmond at about 10:00 a.m. We then went to the baggage claim area, rented a car, and loaded our luggage in the trunk. Connie opened the driver-side door and sat behind the wheel only to discover that she was unable to see over the steering wheel. Therefore, we had to go back and get another car.

We left the airport at about 11:00 a.m. and arrived at the office of the president of Virginia Union University (VUU), hoping we would meet the head of development for the university. To our surprise, her office was two blocks away. We finally found it and were told she was on the main campus for a luncheon. We got back in the car and drove to the building where she planned to dine.

When we finally met her there, she appeared surprised. I introduced myself, and her jaw dropped. I had called her a few days earlier to ask for an accounting of the scholarship. She had not actually entered the dining area when she told me to wait a moment, and that she would go to her office to get the information. When she returned, she came back with a one-page account of some data that was disappointing and not satisfactory to me because there was no indication that any students had been awarded money from my scholarship fund for three years. Moreover, it was not even listed in the college catalogue as a financial opportunity for needy students.

The acting president of the university invited us to lunch, but we declined and continued our journey to Farmville, about sixty miles away. After we unpacked, I decided to visit Prince Edward High School (formerly the Robert Russa Moton High School). Upon arrival, I met with the guidance counselor to see if she had any communication with VUU about my scholarship, and she said, "No," but showed me the current list of scholarships offered by VUU. My scholarship was not on the list! I explained to the guidance counselor that I had just come from visiting VUU, and was told that the scholarship list "had not been updated" since it was established in 2013.

Later that day, we decided to visit Moton H.S., which is now the Robert Russa Moton Civil Rights Museum, a national landmark. I was shocked and amazed to see how it had been transformed into a modern civil rights museum: the building where I had gone to high school from 1939 to 1944 and where from 1948 to 1950 I taught science before entering the Army to serve in the Korean War.

The basic structure of the building had not changed: eight classrooms and an auditorium that seated about 200 students. My wife and I were so impressed with what we saw that we decided to go back the next day. I had taught many of the students involved in the student walkout in 1951, and knew the many civic leaders who fought to change the separate and unequal treatment of both students and teachers during that time.

Later that evening, after a long day, I discovered that all my medicine was missing. I thought perhaps I had left it in the rental car in Richmond. Unfortunately, I was not able to take my pills that night, but the next morning, we went to the CVS pharmacy to have them replaced. While the pharmacists were getting approval to replace my medicine, I took time to visit the nearby Odd Fellows Cemetery to visit the graves of my deceased relatives, including my father, some of my brothers and their spouses, and my sister.

Later that morning, we were invited by the director of the Moton Museum Scholarship Committee to discuss the Family Challenge, an effort to raise funds for the descendants of students who were unjustly deprived of an education from 1959-1964. These funds are intended to provide scholarships to qualified and needy students from PEC to go to college. We made a family donation and are still involved in raising money to help the cause.

The first Moton Museum scholarship recipients entered college in the fall of 2017.

After leaving the meeting that Friday afternoon in Five Forks, we headed to the Styles Family Reunion hosted by my niece and nephew, Shirley and Carl Styles, and their respective families. Upon my father's death, Carl inherited a forty-five-acre farm where the festivities were held. This is where I was born, and my old homestead is still on the property, albeit overgrown now by vegetation.

The fish fry dinner that Carl and Shirley held was a welcoming reception for family and guests. The fish tasted better than any restaurant could prepare because Carl's friends were professional chefs. Music was playing, and a play area had been set up for the kids. There were two long tables brimming with soul food: corn bread, pig's feet, macaroni and cheese, collard greens, ribs, fried chicken, and corn. I had not had pig's feet for many years, and it tasted good. We left about 9:00 p.m. and returned to our hotel room exhausted from the long day.

The following morning, we awakened early to make a reservation at a restaurant named Charley's, which overlooked Buffalo Creek in downtown Farmville. The creek was where my friends and I used to swim. Interestingly, I was informed by one of my relatives that inside the restaurant was a huge scale that was used to weigh slaves during slavery. I had no idea that Farmville was a slave trading location, and my relative shared with me the emotional impact that standing on the inoperative scale had on her. She said it transported her back to slave trading days when families were separated from one another and experienced unimaginable horrors and atrocities after arriving in America. She said that the institution of slavery had a lasting, negative impact on the educational, social, cultural, and economic development of African American families in PEC to this day.

The luncheon we attended was in honor of three classmates and I who graduated from Moton H.S. in 1944: Mary Francis Bell Watkins, Hilda Johnson Cosby, and Ruth Allen Watkins. Due to walking problems and other ailments, they all were accompanied by a guardian. It was a glorious occasion. Everyone was dressed in their finest outfits, and we talked about "old times" that brought back fond memories from seventy-two years ago. A reporter from the *Farmville Herald* greeted us and interviewed me. I told him about the bond we four had formed and that we had also reunited in Farmville in 2008. When he wanted to know why my family contributed to the Moton Museum Scholarship Fund, I replied, "I AM A SON OF PRINCE EDWARD COUNTY and despite everything I have been through, it is still my home."

The luncheon was over at 1:00 p.m. on Saturday, and we drove to Carl's home where the main reunion was taking place. The weather conditions were ideal: warm and sunny but not overbearing. The atmosphere of love was undeniable and overwhelming. We were greeted by twelve tables covered with purple tablecloths. On each table were beautiful, yellow flowers similar to flowers in Carl's home garden. Upon arrival, there was a welcome table headed by my niece, Bunny, from New Jersey, and her daughter, Tahira. They gave everyone a raffle ticket, and a laminated fan that had my father's picture on one side and my deceased brothers and sisters on the other. The inscription on front of each fan was as follows:

PETER AND BERTHA STYLES
Our Family is a circle
Of strength and love
 With every birth and every union
The circle will grow
Every joy shared adds more love
 Every Crisis faced together, makes the circle stronger.

On the back of each fan was written the following:

Friday, August 5, 2016
*Meet & Greet 4:00 p.m.
*Fish Fry
*Story Telling
*Camp –out under the stars
_____-

Saturday, August 6, 2016
*Memorial Service-1:00 p.m.
*Games, Door Prizes and Fellowship
(Horseshoes, Bouncy House, Tug-of-War, Snow cones,
Potato Sack Race, Dominoes,
Checkers and Board Games)
* Dinner—4:00 p.m.
* Shooting Range

The relatives were all gracious and wanted to know who was related to whom. I cannot say enough about how wonderful the coordinators of this reunion were. I am sure countless emails and phone calls were exchanged between my nieces and nephews Carl, Sabrina, Shirley, Dwight, and a host of others in preparation for this two-day event.

As the party was winding down and some people with children were leaving, a lady came over and introduced herself by saying, "I am your niece, and these are my teenage daughters." Well! Not one to ever be at a loss for words, my stunned silence was deafening. After I regained my composure, I asked her about her genealogy. Apparently, my father had had a love child with a neighbor of ours, Miss Jenny Scott. Jenny moved to Lynchburg, Virginia, where she raised my paternal half-sister. She said her mother passed away in 2015 at ninety-seven years of age. Sadly, I never had an opportunity to meet my half-sister but was delighted meet my niece and her family for the first time. We talked for an hour and exchanged telephone numbers. Ever since I met her, we have kept in touch by cell phone, emails, and letters. She attended the 95th birthday celebration of my sister-in-law, Minnie (my late brother Calvin's wife), on October 21st, 2017, in Baltimore. Our family circle now embraces and includes her and her children.

HUMBLE BEGINNINGS

I was the youngest in a family of eight children: six boys and two girls. My father's job as a linesman for the Virginia Electric Power Company (VEPCO) required that he live in Farmville during the week. I vividly remember how my father on Saturdays would hitch a ride ten miles from Farmville to Prospect, Virginia, and then walk or catch a ride from Prospect to our home in Five Forks, carrying a full bag of groceries on his back. My family ate well. He made sure his children always ate healthy, balanced meals. Each Saturday, we looked forward to seeing him because he was like Santa Claus coming to the house with a sack of groceries and goodies on his back.

Over the course of my youth, he learned a lot about electricity and grew in knowledge and stature in the community. He learned how to do things well. He always said that, "A hungry child will steal, and a thief will kill." Best of all, he learned how to get along with people and to stay away from unsavory characters.

Peter Styles, my father, was born in 1892. In those days, elders rarely went past the fourth grade in school because they went to work on farms. Most of the families were large, and children labored in the fields to help support their family. My father was very smart and skillful with his hands.

He learned to read, write, and figure, which became a habit he retained for the rest of his life. He read everything he could lay his hands on such as the *Richmond Times Dispatch, Norfolk Journal and Guide, Baltimore Afro-American Newspaper,* and *The Farmville Herald.* I can proudly say that my father was a man of strength, courage, compassion, integrity, and wisdom.

He generously made time to read to friends and relatives who did not have the opportunity to learn to read. No one could accuse him of being lazy or disrespectful. He was always careful with his money, industrious, and kind with unfailingly good manners. He was a no-nonsense person and never started a fight but was always ready to defend his family and his dignity. "Pa," as we often referred to my father, was a skilled electrician and linesman.

In those days, VEPCO was responsible for bringing electricity to many of the small towns and villages that did not have electricity. In fact, I was told that he and a man named Slate were responsible for extending electric lines ten miles from Farmville to Prospect. In those days, "cherry-pickers" had not been invented. He and his coworkers had to climb cedar electric light poles with cleats on their boots to repair transformers and downed lines. Strong winds, snowstorms, lightning, and automobile accidents could down poles and interrupt electric services for days or even weeks. Whatever the situation, he had to answer the call of his job. At an early age, I was afraid that he would never return because of the danger of being electrocuted by hot wires. At age five-and-one-half, I was old enough to understand that one could be electrocuted if one or one's colleagues made a mistake. My greatest fear back then was that he would leave home and never return. Some weeks he would be gone for periods of two or three days before we heard from him. Living with such fear at this age was traumatic because I knew how much my father meant to me and how he cared for his family. He wanted all eight of his children to succeed and have a good quality of life: Education was his clarion call for all of us. Thinking ahead about our family's future and wellbeing, he often said he did not want us to dig ditches, clean streets, or work as sharecroppers.

We moved from Five Forks because he realized that the school system was not conducive to raising and educating a family. Moving also meant that he would not have to commute from Farmville to Five Forks on weekends to see us, which was difficult. During the week, he lived in Farmville and would come home on weekends to bring food and check on the family. He always instilled in us the importance of getting a good education, saving our money, and not letting anyone "piss on you."

Most people in Five Forks were illiterate farmers who worked for a living day-to-day and year-to-year. Many of them raised chickens, hogs, and tobacco. In the summer, most people cultivated gardens and crops, and canned fruits and vegetables to sustain themselves through the winter. My sister Leora was an avid canner.

ANCESTORS

I was born on a farm in Five Forks, Virginia, on May 18, 1927, in Prince Edward County, Virginia. As mentioned previously, Five Forks is not a town or village. Amazingly, it was not even on the map when I was growing up. It is located at the intersection of Prospect and Hampden-Sydney Roads between Pamplin and Farmville, Virginia. Five Forks was known to be an area where mostly uneducated farmers and poor people lived.

My heritage is somewhat complicated, as well as interesting—not uncommon for that era. The Styles family oldest known ancestor, Aaron Lindsey, was a man known to be an Englishman. We believe Aaron was born in 1805 in PEC and was a landowner of considerable wealth. He married a woman named Livonia, and they had six children, one of whom was my grandfather, Tom. We do not know who our grandmother was because in those days vital statistics were maintained in people's Bibles.

My father, Peter, and his brother Twitty were the sons of Tom and Livonia. The union of Tom's brother, Marcus, with a black woman, gave rise to the Hendricks branch of the family and the union of Tom's sister, Rebecca, with a black man, gave rise to the Scott branch of the family. The union between Marcus and a black woman was annulled. We do not know what happened to my grandfather's other siblings, Frankie and Matthew, but we do know that Tom, Rebecca, and Marcus were ostracized from white society because of their relationships with people of color. In the state of Virginia during this time, it was against the law for a black or white to marry each other based on the Supreme Court case, *Pace v. Alabama*, 106 U.S. 583 (1883), which was finally overturned in 1967 by the Supreme Court case of *Loving v. Virginia,* 388 U.S. 1 (1967).

How did my father, Peter, get the surname Styles? The Lindsey family, for reasons that are not known, gave away my father, Peter, and his brother Twitty to the Styles family (who were black). However, we know of no records of a family with the name of Styles in PEC. We know Peter was Tom Lindsey's son, and we have reason to believe that his mother was named Lucy Freeman, but we don't know who Lucy Freeman was: whether she was black or white and where she came from. However, we do know that Tom and Lucy's union produced Peter and Twitty, after whom I am named. During those days, records were not accurately kept, and therefore, it is hard to trace my ancestry.

At that time, children were shifted around from pillow to post with relatives and friends, and as I just said, accurate records were not kept. Additionally, such family sharing and co-mingling was a hush-hush subject not to be discussed. My father, Peter, was raised by a black family, and although his skin was white, and he had piercing sky blue eyes, his mind, heart, and soul were black. In fact, "black blood" ran through his arteries, veins, and capillaries. He never thought of himself as a white man, even though he could have passed for white (and biologically he was). When I was around five-years-old, I remember visiting my grandfather Tom and his brother Marcus on their farms. They treated us in a cordial and welcoming manner. Pa never raised us to see color: only to accept people as they presented themselves to us.

My father was loving in his own way—not mushy—but strong in looks and deeds. We knew we were loved because of the attention he gave to us.

He was an excellent provider and made sure we had enough food, clothing, and necessities. He was observant and checked on us all the time. He was a worldly man with plenty of experience who passed on to us many wise pieces of advice.

FIVE FORKS

My first five years of life were spent in a home surrounded by forty-five acres of land owned by my father. Pa also owned about fifty-six wooded acres about a mile away. He inherited it from his only brother, Twitty. Tragically, Twitty died on my birthday, May 18, 1927, from typhoid fever.

My name originally was Winfield Junius Styles but upon the death of my uncle, Twitty, my father had my name changed to Twitty. Thus, I became Twitty J. Styles. My father died in 1962, and unfortunately that fifty-six acres inherited from his brother Twitty lead to a shattering of what I once believed to be a tight-knit family. The process of resolving his estate caused a protracted and painful separation, dissention, and loss of communication amongst many of his surviving family. Lawyers had to be hired because some of his grandchildren tried to administer the estate, even though my brother Calvin and I were the principal heirs. The land dispute was eventually taken to court, and a judge finally settled the case. This was an awful time for our family because the bonds of love we all shared before my father's demise were severely strained. Throughout the years, I had heard horror stories about how other families experienced emotional pain, deception, separation, selfishness, and bickering over the family's inheritance of land but never dreamed this could happen in our family. Unfortunately, for us, it did.

With regard to my mother, during the thirties, there were no cures for many contagious diseases such as tuberculosis, whooping cough, and measles. Tragically, when I was three-years-old, my mother, Bertha Ford, died from kidney failure in 1930. I can't recall her facial features or much about her, but soon after my mother's passing, my father hired a nanny named Daisy Pie who, along with my sisters, took very good care of me. Of the eight children my mother and father had, I am the only one living today. I am the patriarch of my father's clan and along with my nephew, Dwight, share the problems, joys, sorrows, and happenings to keep us all connected.

PA WAS A REAL MAN

My father stressed to us the importance of "let your conscience be your guide." He also instilled in us at a very early age the importance of taking advantage of every opportunity afforded to us. Lastly, he told us to be responsible for our behavior and deeds.

I always looked up to Pa. He always taught us right from wrong and to respect elders by using their titles, "Mr." or "Mrs." followed by "please" and "thank you." In those days, married couples respected each other, and when we visited my aunt and uncle on Sundays, I observed that my aunt addressed my uncle as "Mr. Day," and he responded with, "Yes, Mrs. Day?"

On many of those Sundays, my father placed my brother on one shoulder and me on the other, and off we went down the road to visit relatives. Some of my aunts would serve homemade wine to him and cake to us while conversing with each other. My father would always let us take a sip of his wine, so that we would know what is was. After the visit, he would walk home again with my brother and me perched on his shoulders, and then spend the rest of the day preparing for work in Farmville the following day.

When I was thirteen, it was time for me to take off my knickerbocker pants and exchange them for long pants. In those days, this was a rite of passage from being juvenile to being an adolescent. As an adolescent, I did what most youngsters do: I went to school, played with my friends after school, and obeyed my family. My father was a sage. He taught us how to meet and greet folks, look them straight in the eye, smile, and give them a firm handshake, which is a practice that has been passed on to all his grand-children. He always talked about not being lazy and shiftless and how he wanted us to "be somebody." I didn't know what he meant by being some-body in those days, but now I know that he meant for us to be honest, good, productive citizens and to have a better quality of life than he did.

A MOTHERLESS CHILD

On Mother's Day, I often envy people who wear a red rose in honor of their living mother, and a white one for those deceased. I always wear a white one. I don't have any recollection of my mother whatsoever—no photos or anything—because cameras and photographers were few in our town. People who may have had pictures of her are either deceased or have moved away from town. Only the wealthy could afford to have portraits made. As an aside, I bought my first Kodak camera at the PX (Army Post Exchange) while stationed in Tokyo in 1950.

The section of Five Forks we lived in was not so good. It was called "Rattler's Branch," and its economic condition and opportunities to get an education from were very poor. My mother's sister, Aunt Frances, was what you would call poor. She had a family of six children, and they lived in a four-room house that sat on stilts placed among rocks. A strong wind could have blown it down. The walls of her home were papered with colorful comic strips and ads from the newspaper. One could see outside the house through cracks in the wall. We lived in a better area of town, and I did not like it when we occasionally visited her home on Sundays. Despite all of this, she was the most giving woman whom I have ever known. She shared whatever she had with my Pa and our family. As we were leaving, she would say, "Wait a minute, Mr. Styles…" and get eggs, chickens, watermelons, cantaloupes, and vegetables to take home. My father was my hero. In those days, when a parent died, many widowed men gave their families away and parceled them to other relatives or friends to be raised. But, my father didn't do that. I loved him and respected him because he was strong, dedicated, and committed to making sure we that we had a good quality of life.

In the early 1930s, President Roosevelt and his administration passed a rural electrification bill that extended electric power to rural areas of our county and surrounding counties. In those days, people living in rural areas had kerosene lamps, candles, and fireplaces for light. As I mentioned earlier, Pa worked on fallen power lines all over the county. His working attire consisted of knee pants that fitted into boots with cleats to help him climb cedar poles to get to transformers and repair them. He worked year-round, fixing lines after electric storms in the summer and lines damaged by snow and sleet in the winter. I can't recall a time when he took a vacation. He was on call 24/7, and the work was dangerous and exhausting but interesting. Pa often shared his experiences on the job, which gave us a greater appreciation for the work he performed. Pa never used an alarm clock to awaken him for work. His biological clock awakened him on time every day.

We did a lot of shopping at Mr. Turn's country store. In today's jargon, it was a "mini-mall supermarket." It sold everything from gasoline and groceries to dry goods and things country folks needed. It was also a place where town folk met to catch up on news happening in the area. There were no telephones during those days, so going to the store allowed you to get updated on who was in jail, died, had a baby, got married, etc.

My older siblings attended a two-room elementary school, where grades one to four were taught in one room, and grades five to seven in the other room. Although it is not permitted today, I was accompanied by my older siblings to school when I was four. During the times when I could not go to school, "Miss Daisy Pie," my nannie, cared for me.

I had my first encounter with a doctor and nurse around three years of age. My father came home one weekend in the summer and discovered that my pants were sticking to my left side of my behind, and they were hard to remove. He did not know what had happened. He immediately rushed me to a doctor. He discovered that I had suffered a terrible burn on this location. My father asked what I had been playing with, and my older sister, Leora, told him that they had been washing clothes outside under a tree. They had been using a can of lye (sodium hydroxide) as detergent. They had left the can open, and I had sat on it.

I can remember to this day that they had been using a large metal tub with a scrubbing board and octagon soap. I had sat on the can not knowing what it was, and it left the left side of my buttocks scarred for life. The next health professional I saw was a nurse. When I was six years old, I got a shot for diphtheria and tetanus. I can recall the smell of alcohol and antiseptic in the public health clinic office. After that, I don't recall seeing a doctor until I went into the Army.

During the winters, we looked forward to and had fun roasting chestnuts and making ash cakes. They were made from corn meal prepared in eight-inch pancake-like pans placed in the embers of the fire hearth.

When my father came home on weekends, he would check to see if everyone was well. If one of us had a cold, my father would take a spoonful of sugar and add several drops of kerosene oil on top. This was a common home remedy. Kerosene was used many years ago for curative reasons. I also found out that during the Vietnam War, many of the soldiers used kerosene lamps at night. Moreover, I have been told that many of soldiers took a swig of kerosene to get rid of intestinal worms.

CHILDHOOD MEMORIES

It was in the summer of 1932 when we moved from Five Forks to Farmville: I was five. The Great Depression was in full swing, and times were very hard for some people. Pa decided to move the family to Farmville so he wouldn't have to commute on weekends, and he could better care for us. In contrast to living in Five Forks, he was home every night. President Roosevelt had just been elected in 1932, and it was the time of "Happy days are here again…let us sing a song of cheer again…happy days are here again."

When we moved to Farmville, we brought our goat and Irish setter, Bing, a beautiful dog and companion. A few days after arriving, someone stole Bing, and we were traumatized. We had just lost a beloved member of our family.

Despite living during the Depression, we were always well fed, clothed, and cared for. Our rental home did not have a stove in the dining room. In the winter, the dining room and the kitchen were often cold, but my older siblings especially enjoyed making Jell-O there because it would quickly set and be ready to enjoy the next morning. At the time, I was only five and could not enter school that September. I had to wait until the fall of 1932.

Our home in Farmville was located on Ely Street, a thoroughfare for Route 15. We rented our house from the family next door. Our house was an old wooden structure with a parlor, two bedrooms, a dining room, and kitchen with a long hall. At the end of the hall was a small annex that led to a small back porch that had a toilet on the side. It was only a toilet, and not a bathroom. To bathe, we would heat the water on the stove in the kitchen and pour it into a large shiny galvanized tub that was also used to wash clothes in. Heating water on top of the stove in the kitchen was a weekly occurrence on Saturdays. During the other days of the week, we had to take a "bird bath" in order to wash up. Because the house was very drafty and not insulated, there were wood burning stoves in the bedrooms, and each room had a fireplace that provided heat.

Things were difficult for all families during this time. Our first Christmas in Farmville was a thankful celebration. All of us received a paper-tissue-lined shoe box containing colorful hard candy, oranges, walnuts, candy canes, fire-crackers, and sparklers. Next year, my father surprised my brother Calvin and me with sleds. We were proud as peacocks. We usually had plenty of snow during the winter, and there were many hills that didn't have much traffic at the bottoms of them. That Christmas, we frolicked up and down the slopes until midnight and then went home. On Christmas morning, we were served stewed oysters for breakfast. Dinner consisted of T-bone steaks, many starches, and vegetables. We relaxed, sang carols, and enjoyed a great family gathering.

The following year, and each year thereafter, my brother Calvin and 20 of his peers got together at sunset on Christmas Eve and visited South-side Hospital. Despite the temperature being well below freezing, they walked a mile to sing Christmas carols for the patients confined therein. Although the singers were black, law enforcement officers never stopped them. They were entertaining "Mr. Charlie and Miss Ann" (black slang for "white man" and "white" woman), so it was okay.

During the summers, my friend for 85 years, Jimmy Austin, and I made many of our toys. His father had a large horse and wagon with wheels and metal rims. When he discarded the old rims, we saved them and made toys. A bent wire coat hanger would propel the rims up and down the streets. We also spent many hours playing marbles, fiddlesticks, checkers, dominoes, and hopscotch, and flew kites and made fishing poles. Around the corner from Jimmy, a wealthy white family had a large 12-foot concrete wall enclosing their home. It bordered the black neighborhood. Outside of the wall were bamboo trees. We helped ourselves to the bamboo shoots and made fishing poles. We saved enough money to buy tackle, line, and bobbers and had no problems finding large earthworms for bait. We put on our straw hats and off we would go to the creek to fish. We spent many happy hours fishing and swimming in Farmville's Buffalo Creek.

I remember that in the early years of the Great Depression there was a scarcity of coffee, sugar and meat, and that there were blackouts and food rationings. Many people were out of work, and there were lines to get coffee, sugar, and other staples. The Civilian Conservation Corps (CCC) operated from 1933 to 1942 by the federal government to find public works jobs for the unemployed, unmarried men, and many men in Farmville benefited from it.

On another note, my father always told us that "education" was the key to a better quality of life. He felt that one had to finish at least high school. Education was his clarion call, and that call has stayed with me all my life. He said, "I don't care how people treat you and what comes your way: no one can take your education away from you. It is yours." These words were stamped into my psyche then and reside there even today: I continue to learn as much about things as possible because "Pa" made me "hungry" to learn and to help others. Pa often said, "I don't want you digging ditches" and he also emphasized the importance of, "saving your money," not letting anyone "piss on you," and giving back to others. He never disciplined us physically. All he had to do was to give us a certain look. We respected and honored him and tried to make him proud.

On the other hand, I missed my mother, whom I never really knew. Her loss left a certain emptiness in my development. Until I was twelve, I felt like a motherless child, even though my sisters and nannie looked after me. Eventually, my father took a new bride, and as a result, I had a stepmother. At that age, I was an adolescent, and my morals and values had been shaped. His wife was young. In fact, I had a brother older than her. One day his wife threatened to beat me, and I told my older sister, who then told my father that his wife was not to lay her hands on me. My sister kept watch over me and made sure that my stepmother would not threaten to beat me again. It didn't happen again.

As a young person, my father saw something in me that I cannot explain. I was an inquisitive child, and my brothers and sisters would laugh and wonder why I asked so many questions. In first grade, I would always ask questions such as what, where, and why. My father had a premonition about me. On more than one occasion, he told my brothers and sisters: "Don't laugh at that boy. He may have to take care of you before it is over."

I can't explain. He was prophetic and spent most of his free time exposing me to as many "educational" things as possible. After we moved to town, he bought us a radio, and we were able to hear the news, music, soap operas, Amos and Andy, Jack Benny, and President Roosevelt's "fireside chats." I always listened intently and looked forward to the president's radio shows in particular. Although my father subscribed to the *Richmond News Leader* and *Farmville Herald,* and was an avid newspaper reader, there were few books in our home. Pa did not have a lot of formal education but had "mother wit," which can be defined as good common sense.

Pa taught us at an early age to respect others. I can remember things that I witnessed before moving to town when I was five-years-old. During the early 30s, I remember we were a close-knit community where people shared their crops. In December, it was pig-killing time when farmers would get together, slaughter pigs, and share fresh pork with each other. Many farmers also cured ham and shoulder parts to eat at other times during the year. This was an annual tradition that everyone looked forward to. They would put sage, salt, and other ingredients on the meat, smoke it for days, and hang the preserved meats in the smokehouse for later use.

Back in those days, farmers also had sugar cane nights, where they boiled sugar cane and extracted the syrup. Large iron vats filled with water held the sugar cane to boil for hours, and as it cooled down it produced molasses, which went well with corn bread. In the summer, corn, potatoes, beans, sweet potatoes, tomatoes, and all kinds of vegetables were grown. I shall never forget the red cherry tree and the melon and strawberry patches in our yard. We had fun eating the fruit because we could eat as much as we wanted. There was never a shortage of food.

SIBLINGS

Folks living in the country did not have access to or use books to guide their selection of names for their children. This practice sometimes resulted in unusual and creative names for children. This happened in my family. My two oldest brothers were named Luther and Arsenia. My sisters were named Leora and Florence, my twin brothers were named Lawrence and Lloyd, my next oldest brother was Calvin, and I, the youngest, Twitty.

After we moved to Farmville in the early thirties, my eldest brothers, Luther and Arsenia, went to Baltimore to seek employment. My cousin, Willie Ford, and his wife provided them with a room in their home to live in. Luther considered himself a surrogate father to me, and followed my many activities.

MY BROTHERS

LUTHER

Luther worked at Sparrows Point at Bethlehem Steel in Baltimore County for 40 years. He was a labor leader and foreman who retired due to illness in 1970. He watched over me through high school and college, however, and was not arrogant or boastful but cool as a cucumber. It appeared that he was stress free. He was tall, dark, handsome, used a mild smelling after-shave lotion, and always looked like a page out of *Esquire* magazine. He always made sure that his dress clothes were tailored to fit his six-foot-four-inch frame. The ladies went after him like flies looking for flycatcher paper. His demeanor was always that of a Virginia gentleman, and he wore spats (short leather coverings) over his shoes.

When he was forty-five, he met his young wife, Mary, who was the mother of his five sons and one daughter. He provided a good home for his family and made sure his children got a good education. There was a special bond between us. He was the patriarch of the family and now that he is gone, I have replaced him as the head of the family and feel responsible for all of our surviving children and grandchildren.

ARSENIA

Arsenia was the second son. He was also good looking with a copper-brown complexion. His world was shattered, too, when my mother, Bertha, passed on June 6th, 1930. In January of 1943, he was drafted into the Army, and sent to Staten Island, New York. He had a terrible accident on a ship and was wounded badly. Upon recovery, he served in France, Belgium, and finally, Germany. When his tours were over, he returned to Portsmouth, Virginia, and then to Fort Meade, Maryland, where he was honorably discharged.

He suffered from crippling rheumatoid arthritis, however, for over 59 years. It was an uphill battle in the latter part of his life. His oldest son, Leon, served in the Navy and later the Army. Unfortunately, he contracted a parasitic disease and passed away at a very young age. I never had strong connection with Arsenia because he was busy caring for his wife and seven children.

LAWRENCE

I was blessed to have twin brothers: Lawrence and Lloyd. Lawrence got married early and had a son and daughter. He had two jobs—one as a maintenance man for the Virginia Electric Power Company and the other as supervisor of the janitorial service for Farmville Methodist Church. He was deeply involved in the church and loved fishing and hunting during his spare time. He collected antiques such as beautiful vases, an 11th-century organ, and all kinds of bottles and lamps.

He remained in Farmville but suffered from a stroke that paralyzed his left side and incapacitated him for the rest of his life. His last ten years were spent in a nursing home before he passed. Lawrence was always happy to see his brothers and sisters when we came home to visit him.

LLOYD

Lloyd enjoyed wine, women, and song. One day, he met a girl named Eve-lyn, and moved into her home with her parents and sisters. They cohabi-tated together for many years. He had a good job at Sparrows Point and always took me under his wing. He made sure that I didn't need anything while going to school. He had a friend who ran a cleaning and pressing shop. I was temporarily employed to watch his shop and wait on customers. When the boss took a break, I was in charge of the shop. I earned a few bucks for school during that summer.

Lloyd liked his drinks and was a scoundrel until one day something "hit him" and told him that he must change his ways. At that time, he did not at-tend church and was not a Christian. It turned out that he had met a young lady named Annie, and they had started dating. She was a devout Christian and attended a church that some folks considered to be only for "holly rollers." They were very vocal and responded loudly to the pastor's sermons. It was a predominantly black megachurch called "Bible Way," located on Third Street in Washington, D.C. Their services were very long with "fire and brimstone" messages that had women fainting and members running up and down the aisles. Many nurses were on call to "revive" people who had fainted or collapsed in a frenzy and needed to be brought back to reality.

When I was in college, I attended one Sunday, and the Rev. C.L. Franklin from Detroit was the guest preacher. One would have thought the "Holy Ghost" was present: There were so many "Amens," "Yes, sirs," "Come ons," and "Lord, if you pleases" coming from the audience. The most interesting event of that day was when Rev. Franklin introduced his twelve-year-old daughter, Aretha Franklin, the "Queen of Soul," as the guest soloist. She brought the house down with her voice, stage presence, and songs. The wor-ship service lasted over three hours with the money plate passed around about five times for one cause or another. I left there that day never dreaming that

Aretha would someday become a world-famous entertainer, but she did.

After about five years as a member, Lloyd became a deacon and travelled to many churches in the U.S. He completely turned his lifestyle around and accepted the Lord as his savior. No more drinking and fooling around for him. He was especially fond of me, took good care of me, and admired the fact that I was getting an education, an opportunity he did not have when he came along. At the end of his life, he suffered from multiple complications including heart, kidney failure, sleep apnea, and other symptoms. However, he died knowing that he had repented for all his worldly sins and was saved by the Lord.

CALVIN

Calvin left home when he was eighteen. He had finished high school, and the only available work at that time was setting up pins at the local bowling alley and doing menial jobs. One Saturday, he was walking downtown on Main and Third Street in Farmville when a group of white men were blocking his way. In those days, blacks were expected to step aside when whites were walking their way. Calvin did not yield to these men by stepping aside. He walked in between them, and an argument ensued. They reported the incident to the police, and Police Chief Lipscomb suggested that he leave town to avoid further confrontation. He decided to join his older brothers and cousins in Baltimore where he found work with Westinghouse, and later, with Pan American Airways.

After about two years, he met his wife of 64 years. He and Minnie were the proud parents of two girls and four boys. They made sure that all their children received a college education, and now they have families of their own. Calvin worked for the Baltimore City Housing Authority and retired after 38 years of service. He was responsible for oversight and maintenance of thousands of housing units available to city residents through the Baltimore City Housing Authority.

Calvin often sent his children to Farmville to spend time with my father and our step mother. There were many warm, enjoyable summers and holidays spent at the family home. Calvin was three years older than me, and a senior in high school when I was a freshman. His friends were more mature than me, and they hung out together. I used to observe them but was too young to hang out with them. I did not have an ongoing dialogue with most of my brothers because they were older and migrated away from home to start their own journeys. However, as Calvin and I aged, we became close and shared family secrets and business between us. We would often reminisce about old times when we saw each other.

Calvin lived to be 92-years-old. He was a great father and provider. He worked three jobs and made sure his children pursued the dream of higher education as advocated by our father. His wife Minnie just recently celebrated her 95th birthday. Connie and I and all the members of her family and extended family were present. She was Queen for the day with her silver tiara, silver lace gown, and silver-painted fingernails. There were many tributes paid to her, and we all hope to be around when she turns 100.

MY SISTERS

LEORA

Leora, my oldest sister, married Jackson Brown a few years after we moved to Farmville. Leora was my surrogate mom, and I was her pride and joy. We had fun talking about school, church, and relatives. She was a fair-skinned woman with good hair. She knew how to cook, sew, and take care of a home. Jack was a tall, muscular man who lived with his sister a few blocks away. Jack had a niece and nephew around my age, and we played together. Jack worked for the Coca-Cola company and delivered truckloads of refreshments to businesses in the area. One day, Jack's sister moved to New Jersey, and left her children in his care. When Jack and Leora were married, my sister looked after Jack's sister's children, John and Beatrice. Leora stayed at home full-time to care for her niece and nephew in the absence of their mother.

After a few years of marriage, Leora sought work out of the home to supplement their income. This decision would have unintended consequences on her health and the well-being of her young family and loved ones. She was employed as a domestic by a local dentist and his wife. Leora cleaned, cooked, and took care of the couple's daughter, Margaret Ann.

Two years into her employment, she complained about feeling weak, tired, and lethargic. A persistent severe cough developed that was tainted with blood. The doctor diagnosed her illness as an active case of tuberculosis. She was given medicine and confined to a period of bedrest for approximately two years before she started to recover. All the members of her husband's family and the extended family had to be tested. Thankfully, she was the only one positive for tuberculosis (TB), but everyone wanted to know where and how she got it.

We subsequently discovered that the dentist's wife, Ann Sydney, had TB and that she was the source of Leora's infection. Leora was exposed to the bacteria daily and tragically contracted it. She was never told about Ann Sydney's infection.

My sister needed that job to help support her family. If the Sydney's had had the decency to tell her about the TB, she could have taken precautions to minimize her risk of contracting it or found work for another family in town. The dentist was only interested in having someone care for his wife and family. This is an example of how poorly blacks were treated. The family knew of the wife's condition, and no one provided Leora with a mask or gloves to protect her from contracting it. She had to leave her job, and that was the end of her affiliation with the Sydney's. She never heard from her boss or his family after she contracted it – not a call, get well card, or note. Had she known that "Miss Ann" had TB, she would have never taken the job. It was an example of white selfishness and looking out for their own. Leora never had an opportunity to learn about her disease until it was too late. Fortunately, she recovered and was able to live for many years thereafter.

While Leora was getting well, she was strong enough to enjoy watching from her kitchen window her small garden grow. One day, she looked out to see her husband Jack having sex with a neighbor in the garden. She summoned all her strength and grabbed her kitchen broom and a stick and quickly ended Jack's garden tryst. He learned his lesson, and to my knowledge, it did not happen again. There was a price to be paid for his infidelity. Leora was a fearless, loving, and kind sister with a heart of gold. She reminded me of our Aunt Frances who lived in Five Forks and didn't have anything but would give you the shirt off her back.

During Leora's illness, I stopped by every afternoon on my way home from school to spend some time with her. She always was happy to see me and my report card, and would praise me for making the honor roll. She liked that my father stressed education, education, education. Her home was welcome to all members of the family, especially to her nieces and nephews who spent the summers in town. I loved her very much, and she would do anything for me and my family. She suffered a stroke from high blood pressure and died in her late seventies.

FLORENCE

Florence, my younger sister, was married to Eldridge Thompson, a.k.a, Sonny, who used to be a cook at Hampden-Sydney College. They were married in 1939 and shortly thereafter moved to the Bronx in New York City. She joined the Union Baptist Church choir and devoted a lot of time to the church. She was a housewife, and Sonny found a new job as superintendent of two large apartment complexes on Prospect Avenue, which was a tree lined street that used to be the home to rich white people.

His job was to stoke up the furnace with coal in the morning and to be on call to fix the plumbing and make other household repairs. They were blessed with two beautiful daughters, and, when they were old enough for school, Florence got a job working in White Plains, NY, to help supplement their family income. Both of her daughters married and had families of their own. One of them married a minister, and the other married an engineer from the telephone company. Her youngest daughter preceded her in death due to heart problems.

MY STEPMOTHER

Carroll, my stepmother, was the same age as my oldest brother, Luther. I was twelve when my father married her. He was as happy as a clam. She filled a void in his life that had been missing for years. She was a good wife, cook, baker, and seamstress and took care of her home. She was young and vivacious, and liked to dance and shake her hips. She fulfilled his needs. He thought she was a princess, and he treated her like one. She liked new clothes and had good taste in buying fine china, cutlery, stem wear, and silver for their house. She made the best homemade rolls, fried chicken, potato salad, and macaroni and cheese: she liked to cook soul food.

While I was in high school studying and working, this change in my family structure made me feel a bit like an outsider. After they married, Carroll was at the center of his life. Thinking back to that time, although I felt like I was not at the center of Pa's focus, I knew his profound love for me had not changed. He had already instilled in me the moral and social values he wanted me to embrace. I still felt alone, however, and it bothered me. So, I kept busy preparing myself for college. I think she liked me, but her needs came first in our household. The tremendous amount of fat in her southern cooking may have been a factor that contributed to his demise. Today, we all realize the health benefits of a low-fat diet, something that he did not have the opportunity to consume during his marriage with Carroll.

In December 1962, she went shopping, and when she returned, a little after lunch, he had expired from a stroke. I still wonder how much longer he would have lived without her artery- clogging dishes. I was at NYU, finishing up work on my doctorate when the news came. I was shocked and devastated but knew that I had to be strong during those days. I felt that he had imparted all the wisdom and advice he had to give, and I had returned his love every time I had an opportunity. I still have not been able to deal with his death. I know that life goes on, however. I have also felt his presence (like a "hawk watching a chicken," we used to say) at certain times during my life's journey. When I called my sister Florence, who lived in the Bronx, to tell her about his death, she was so distraught at the news that she yanked the telephone from the wall and threw it out the kitchen window. I had to drop everything and rush to console her.

MOTON ELEMENTARY SCHOOL

The first school I attended was Robert Russa Moton School. It accommodated grades one through seven on the first floor and grades eight through eleven on the second floor. Because so many children had to help work the farms, teachers emphasized the importance of hygiene and good eating habits daily. In first grade, the teacher had a health wall chart with everyone's name on it. There were columns labeled at the top listing hair, teeth, nails, and other things to encourage you to come to school clean. I remember the smell of Lifebuoy soap, which pervaded the classroom, and suggested your family practiced good health habits. Gold stars were given to the students who met the criteria for cleanliness each day. Believe me, my friends and I worked hard to get gold stars each day. This was my first introduction to health education.

Once a week, we had an assembly in the school auditorium. We lined up and marched to the music of John Philip Sousa. We sang patriotic songs, and occasionally there was a speech by the principal and announcements about school business. In third grade, I studied geography and loved it because we discussed the continents, the nations in the world and its many cultures. Our teacher always had us dress up like people from areas such as Africa, Holland, Japan, and South America. This was fascinating. I never dreamed that someday I would have an opportunity to visit countries in Europe, Asia, Africa, and South America. I look back today and think, "You have come a long way, baby, in spite of all of the ingrained racism, sexism, and negative forces around you."

Our teachers taught us to respect each other and to study, study, study. They understood that education was and is the only way to improve the quality of one's life. Unfortunately, we did not have any athletic equipment or a gym. We would spend twenty minutes outside after lunch to get some fresh air, and that was it. As a result, I never became a good athlete. On another note, I remember that the school held a spring cantata that students participated in and parents attended.

My elementary school education was fostered by a caring group of black teachers who gave us all they could to help us work towards a better quality of life and to make a difference in the lives of others. We were the future, and they wanted us to be the best we could be despite an educational environment where supplies and facilities were inadequate, unequal, crowded, and meager.

Although the climate for learning was substandard, we still learned the basics: reading, writing, and arithmetic. My first-grade reader was *Dick and Jane*. It was a standard book about little white boys and girls. In the third grade, I remember that we sang an operetta for the parents:

> *"I am robin red bird, the forerunner of spring…the winter knows its spell is over when I begin to sing… I truly am, I do believe, the original early bird, and I could tell of worms I have caught but that's another word…"*

Although my elementary days were uneventful, routine, and not exciting, I spent seven years there from the first grade onward. Each day we had to march in a single file. I still remember the piano playing one of Sousa's patriotic march songs such "Stars and Stripes" or James Bland's "Carry Me Back to Old Virginny" as we marched to class. There is one line that I still remember from the chorus:

"Carry me back to old Virginny,
There's where the cotton and the corn and taters grow;
There's where the birds warble sweet in the springtime;
There's where this old darkey's
heart am long'd to go."

We sang this song once or twice a week in the auditorium but were unaware of its racial undertones. After announcements were made, it was time to sing. This was our only exposure to music.

In those days, there were "bullies" who tried to beat up kids and intimidate them. I had an older boy in my class who was much larger and stronger than me. He would not let anyone touch or put their hands on me. I felt like he was my guardian angel.

THE THIRTIES

I was a student of the Prince Edward County (PEC) school system from grades one through eleven. Grade twelve was added later. The education system in the PEC system was separate and unequal, and the Moton High School case was one of five cases that coalesced into the *Brown v Board of Education* suit brought before the Supreme Court to integrate and make the PEC system equitable.

In the 1930s, there were approximately 14,520 residents in PEC, fifty percent black and fifty percent white. Prior to 1930, the county offered black students nothing beyond an elementary education. In 1939, I finished elementary school and started high school at Moton High School. It had just been completed and built with funding from the local public administration. It was no secret that the public white school received more funding than ours.

In high school, I was president of the junior and senior classes. We had no middle school. To graduate and go to college, there was a distribution requirement: I think we had to earn sixteen credits consisting of English, mathematics, science, foreign language, and civics.

After completing college, I was hired as a science teacher at Moton High, and enrollment started showing signs of increasing. The school was built to accommodate 180 students, but due to the burgeoning enrollment over my two-year tenure, the student population exceeded 450 students. When I was teaching there, my first year's pay was $1,800.00. Later that year, I was awarded a Westinghouse Science Teacher's Fellowship to study at the Massachusetts Institute of Technology (MIT) over the summer. The goal of the Westinghouse was to improve the teaching of science and mathematics in high schools and to encourage and prepare for college high school students interested in science. I spent the summer at M.I.T. and then started my second academic year at Moton from 1949-1950. I thoroughly enjoyed teaching, but was soon drafted into the Army in 1950 to fight in the Korean conflict. I proudly answered the call of Uncle Sam to serve my country.

A year after I left the States for military service, tensions between whites and blacks and their separate schools in PEC began to boil over. Because I grew up in the Farmville school system and experienced firsthand its separate and unequal conditions, I understood why on April 23, 1951, 16-year-old Barbara Johns, niece of Rev. Vernon Johns, farmer, preacher, and civil-rights pioneer, led 450 Moton students to protest the inequality of educational opportunities for black students in Farmville, Virginia. Some historians consider her protest to be the start of the civil rights movement in the U.S., as it was the only one of the five cases in *Brown v. Board* that was led by students. Moton High School today is known as the Moton Museum and Center for the Study of Civil Rights.

THE FORTIES

My class was the second one to enter the new R.R. Moton High School at the intersection of Ely and Main Streets in Farmville. In high school, we had a homeroom teacher and several class periods during the day. Between each period, a bell rang and you had about five minutes to go from room to room and take care of your bodily needs. There was a time schedule for each class, with about forty-five minutes allotted for lunch. There was no time for physical education or any other activities. My older brother, Calvin, was a senior, and I was a freshman, a newcomer. There was no communication among seniors and underclassmen—they were three years older, and it made a difference at that age. I went to each class and spent a lot of time in the library, where I was able to read many books and keep up with current events. We compared grades with each other at the end of each marking period and were very competitive.

Outside of the classroom, I spent time as a newspaper boy, a golf caddy, an ice-hauler, a yard-raker, and a worker at Chappell's Fountain and Book-store downtown. Sometimes, I spent my lunch period walking two blocks away to McKnight's service station and restaurant where my friends and I ate hamburgers, hot dogs, cheeseburgers, coca-colas, potato chips, and large, red delicious apples.

I had five buddies in high school, and we used to hang out together. We worked to pay for some of our clothing, we played cards on Sundays, and we would meet after school to talk about current events and girls. The closest black college was Virginia State College in Petersburg, approximately an hour and a half away by train from Farmville. In the fall of our junior and senior years in high school, we all attended a college football game in Petersburg. We took a segregated train down in the morning and returned later the same day. That was our first introduction to college students, coeds, and sophisticated groups of people. It was fun, and we always talked about going to college after graduation. We were introduced to college life there, but I was never interested in attending a state school. I was attracted to a private school, like VUU, because the students whom I knew there were more sophisticated and seemed more studious.

Many of my friends were drafted into the service in the early 40s, and I lost several who sacrificed their lives for our country. Furthermore, many of our high school teachers took days off, and that meant we had substitutes who didn't teach much; instead, they just kept order. It created a gap in our studies because most subs were simply not teaching anything, and we students paid the price.

During the early 40s, WWII was raging, resources were rationed, blackout drills were common, and we spent a lot of time listening to music and to the fights of Joe Louis. He was a national hero for blacks, and for people in general. Despite all the things we could not do, we enjoyed the Big Band era. We learned how to identify the bandleaders, their theme songs, and the various instruments played. Each week, we listened and learned the lyrics of the Hit Parade of songs on the radio. The songs were rated from one to twenty-five. I remember that McKnight's had a jukebox that I stuffed with coins to listen to popular bands and current music.

Recently, PBS broadcasted two segments on jazz that showed how many white bands and musicians had taken over music that long had roots in the black community. It was during the 1940s that black bands led by Duke Ellington, Earl Hines, Louis Armstrong, and others followed the Chitlin' Circuit (a series of concert venues where blacks could perform in relative safety). They played at the famous Apollo Theater in Harlem and at well-known venues in Philadelphia, Baltimore, Washington, D.C., and down the east coast to Florida. They were not allowed to stay or eat in white motels or hotels—only in black lodges or boarding houses. In fact, I remember that one evening Farmville hosted the "The International Sweethearts of Rhythm"—an all-black female band who played at our Elks Hall.

The International Sweethearts of Rhythm were the first integrated all-women's band during the 1940s. They featured some of the best female musicians in the world, and during the feminist movements of the 1960s and 1970s, they were very popular, particularly with lyricists and musicologists. Their goal was to show that women could contribute to the evolution of jazz music, too!

I was too young to go inside the hall, but my friends and I could hear them from outside. We clapped our hands and watched the adults shaking their hips, doing the jitterbug, and grinding away on the slow songs. We also noticed through the windows that some of the men wore zoot suits and conked their hair by using a straightening compound. It worked for some men but gave others severe burns to their scalps.

My school pals and I used to save our money to buy recordings of the big bands and get together to discuss the merits of their music. Our favorite vocalists at the time were Billy Holiday, Ella Fitzgerald, Sarah Vaughn, and Diana Washington. My cousin, Bill Ford, played saxophone with the famous "Cootie" Williams. Black bands performed, entertained, and earned a living from music in the 40s, but they did not receive the recognition they deserved or the equitable income they deserved.

In the segregated south of the 40s, discrimination was common place. Blacks were restricted as to where they could eat or lodge. In fact, there were signs along the route that read "Eat Nigger Chicken." If blacks wanted something to eat, their food had to be taken out of the restaurant and given to them. There were "Whites only" and "Blacks only" signs everywhere.

Mr. McKnight, a black owner of a service station in Farmville, spent part of the winters in Florida and some of his summers in Manchester, Vermont. He had a connection with a hotel chain that needed cheap labor for summer help. Each summer he would take some high school students to the *Equinox House*, a resort for the rich and famous located in Manchester, Vermont. One summer, I went with him and some other students to work as a houseman. I set up rooms for guests and made sure that the furniture was just right, the curtains were in place, the flowers in the room were watered, and that everything was clean and in impeccable order.

Miss Robbins was head of housekeeping. She was about fifty-five with gray hair and spoke very rapidly with a New England accent. She was a bit eccentric, as she would run up and down the halls looking for me and calling me in her high-pitched voice, "Julius. Now, Julius. Where are you?" (I was always in the next room checking everything that she had just checked.) Nonetheless, she was good and kind to me and recommended me for a job in Miss Lipman's jewelry shop. My job was to polish the silver for the patrons who would be spending lots of money there. I also caddied for guests during the afternoons. It was hard work, but I earned decent money from tips, got three meals a day, and had a place to stay.

Miss Robbins was also known as "Miss Quality Control." White maids took care of cleaning the rooms and removing the sheets and towels. I met two of them, and they told me that they were from Schenectady, New York. I had never heard of Schenectady nor could I pronounce it. They spent their summers in Vermont and returned home after the season ended. I never thought that in a million years I would end up working in Schenectady, but I eventually did. It is amazing how connected life experiences are.

Mr. McKnight's wife, Maida, was a member of the Martha E. Forrester Council of Colored Women. She was a civic leader who was on the battlefield doing all she could to improve the schools and provide students with a good education. She organized a quiet, under the radar group of intelligent farmers and professionals whom she made aware of the injustices in the educational system. As the wife of a businessman, she knew that only self-employed members of the community could speak out. If employed by a white person, one had to be silent for fear of losing his job or being penalized in other ways: people were always aware of the racial hierarchy. Many whites realized the separate but unequal situation they were a part of and may have sympathized with us but could not openly express their opinions.

The school strike in 1951 brought people together to fight for equal school facilities. This unrest just didn't happen but had been simmering for years and people could not talk about it. Black people worked for whites yet many of them were "Uncle Toms" and "Aunt Tomasinas": moles who told their white employers everything they knew about "troublemaking blacks." These sellouts thought that white people loved them. They helped keep us in our so-called "place" for years, and things would be that way today, or worse, had the strike not occurred.

Speaking of strikes, a *Lucky Strike* cigarette salesman would stand about a block from our school and hand out a small packet of free cigarettes to try to get the boys hooked. My friends and I did not fall for it and just ignored him. I never became a smoker.

SUMMERS AND PART- TIME WORK

On holidays and school closings, my friends and I would carry luggage for the female students from Longwood College to the bus and train stations. One could make several trips and earn between fifty cents and one dollar for each one.

We looked forward to college vacations days and the opportunity to carry the students' luggage: it provided the funds we used to go to the balcony of the segregated Lee Theater to watch movies and to buy records and school supplies. There were no recreation centers in town for blacks, so we spent Saturdays going to see double-features starring Gene Autry, Hop-a-Long Cassidy, Roy Rogers, Buck Jones, Flash Gordon, and "Ming the Merciless."

Following our weekly Saturday afternoon matinees, we went home satiated with cinema until the following weekend. During summer vacations, we would also go fishing, play marbles or baseball, and make kites and other toys to play with. During some Saturdays, we would sit on the main post office steps hoping to be asked by a doctor, lawyer, or affluent person if we could caddie for them. They would drive us about three miles out of town, where the eighteen-hole golf course was located, and some of their bags would be heavier and larger than us. We did not mind because it was an honest way to earn money. In case we encountered a poisonous snake, we took a golf club with us when we looked for the balls that ended up in the rough.

After spending over three hours on the course, we would clean the clubs, put them in the back of the car, and be "paid" forty-five cents and a bottle of cola. We didn't complain because we were glad to have some pocket change. I knew most of the players by face because they visited Chappell's store, where I worked for four years to earn money for college. I saved a lot of my hard-earned money and can't remember <u>not</u> working. When I earned a dollar, I held on to it until "the eagle hollered" at me to spend it.

Work was my middle name. I have always had a job since I was thirteen: I received my first social security card at that age. My father taught us to work hard, save our money, get a good job, and "don't let anybody piss on you." This advice has served me well in trying to reach the goals I have set for myself. I have served as a newspaper carrier, baggage carrier, golf caddy, yard-raker, lawn-mower, waiter, and NYC Health Department worker. At thirteen, I also had a paper route with about thirty customers. It was not at all lucrative because some weeks the customers did not pay, even though I had to pay for the papers. It was very stressful, so I gave it up. My buddy Jimmy and I, whom I have known for eighty years, worked together as a team.

On one Saturday, close to Halloween, we walked through an upscale neighborhood to find work to earn money to go to the movies. So, we went to the back door of "Miss Ann's" home. She had a large lawn, and we hoped to mow and rake and earn enough to go to the matinee and buy a bag of popcorn. We spent three hours cutting and manicuring her lawn. At noon, "Miss Ann" came out of her back door and handed each of us four cookies. It felt as if we had been tricked, not treated. We needed to earn fifteen cents each to go to the afternoon matinee, but she gave us only cookies. That was a scarring hurt. She took advantage of us because we were little black boys.

I also recall later in my life when I was a doctoral student at NYU, I took a job at a business that stretched curtains for the big hotels on Park Avenue, Central Park South, and for other first-class establishments in Manhattan. The job was in Astoria, Queens, on Long Island. I remember working from 4:00 p.m. until midnight. The starched curtains were washed in the laundry and then had to be stretched by hand on metal racks that contained short pins. I had to use my knuckles to secure them on the rack, and the pins made tiny holes in my hands that were very painful. I still have scars from the pins penetrating my flesh. This kind of hard work forged my character, determination, and resilience.

ENCOUNTER WITH LAW ENFORCEMENT

I had my first encounter with the criminal justice system in Farmville when I was a teenager. One night, the Police Chief and two officers were at the train station. He was a six-foot tall, imposing person with a moustache. He also wore a large cap and long blue coat. The kids would make fun of him by saying, "Tall man, blue coat, put me in the mind of a Billy goat." In those days, "Mr. Charlie" was a term used for white men in positions of authority and "Miss Ann" for women. It was expected by them to be addressed by blacks in this manner. On the other hand, it did not matter how old or what station in life black men had achieved, most southern whites referred to them as "boy," with no name or title.

My encounter with Chief Lipscomb came one day when he asked me, "Boy, what is your name?" I told him, and he said, "I want you to come down to the sheriff's office next Monday at 8:00 a.m." I told my father, and he took me down and waited outside. Chief Lipscomb admonished me for trying to make some pocket change by serving as a porter for the Longwood women. Next, he told me to put some logs in the wood box, and then he let me leave for school. That was my first and only encounter with the criminal justice system: one that I shall never forget. I was only a thirteen-year-old trying to make a buck. That is another scar that is unforgettable.

CHAPPELL'S BOOK STORE

I entered high school in 1939, and my class was the second to go to the "new" school. I worked mornings, afternoons, and all-day Saturday for four years at Chappell's Fountain and Book Store on Main Street, where the movers and shakers in Farmville went to renew their energy, shop, and get the latest gossip. The store was divided into two parts: on the left side, there was a soda fountain and sandwich shop with a few booths and some tables, and on the right side, they sold books, candy, cigars, cigarettes, and stationery supplies. There was no division of labor: I did everything from making chicken and ham salad sandwiches to scrubbing the floor, washing the windows, restocking the shelves, serving coffee, and answering the telephone. I was happy to let other employees make change and handle the money because if money came up short, I did not want to be accused of stealing.

For all the time and energy I devoted to this store, I was paid the sum of one dollar and fifty cents for the week. I was smart enough to know what child labor laws were and knew that in my case, they had been violated. But, I was trapped. I had tried to save the money I earned each week because the bank was only a few yards from the store, and I wanted to go to college. At that time, I had to buy my own used books with no discount. I did not know how to address this unjust situation, but I knew that for a fact that the store was exploiting my labor—yet another scar in my psyche that I carry with me today. People don't understand why I sometimes react the way I do in certain situations. It's because I was exploited when I was younger. I don't let others attempt to cheat or exploit me now. I don't hesitate to challenge someone who attempts to cheat me—a life's lesson learned the hard way. I act with honesty in my transactions with others and expect the same honesty to be returned to me.

When one has no recourse or power, one must keep one's mouth shut, ears open wide, and keep on trucking. I was tired and weary at that age, but I kept remembering the old hymn, titled, "There is a bright side somewhere." The only things that sustained me in those days were Sunday School, the Baptist Young Peoples Union, and encouragement from family and friends. I still remember many Bible verses and old Negro spirituals from my childhood. When I get sick, lonely, or depressed, I strike up a hymn and start singing. All I do is hum a verse, and things get better.

Black students never were sold the first edition of books at Chappell's. Our books had been used by white students and were handed down. I did have the privilege of choosing the best used books, however. I took pride in my books, despite their used condition, and covered them using a brown paper bag with some glue.

The thing that has remained with me all my life is how hard I worked at Chappell's but was never recognized as person. I had to wear a white cap and an apron, and played the role of the nice but "invisible" boy with no feelings. When I look back, because of the harsh treatment I received, I amassed power and inner-strength that one can only learn from such an experience. Those days prepared me to be multi-dimensional at a very young age. They also taught me how to read a person's body language and to anticipate where he or she may be going. I think that's one reason I have been able to survive and persevere in encounters with all kinds of people. Having been an invisible object at Chappell's, my ears were filled with the venom, hatred, and prejudice that spewed like fiery dragons from some white people's mouths: "nigger...darky...coon...crow... sambo..." and other derogatory comments were regularly made about blacks, and sometimes about me. The words they used were stereotyping blacks as lazy, easy-going, shiftless, and dumb. The origin of the term "sambo" arose with the publishing of a book written by Helen Bannerman in 1889, a white English woman. The book describes a dark-skinned boy's child adventures with four tigers. *Little Black Sambo* received great popularity in America. Many people believe that the popularity of it was due to an acceptance of racism and a distorted fascination with stereotyped images of blacks presented by the entertainment industry.

The customers at Chappell's did not know that I was smart enough to understand what they were saying nor did they care. I was invisible. Despite all the bigotry and hurtful words I heard, I was able to save up five hundred dollars to help me defray the expenses of my first year at VUU. I always felt that in time, a change would come, and it did.

My boss at Chappell's married a woman who worked next door at Baldwin's Department Store. She liked me and would let me purchase things on a lay-away plan. Because I was six-feet, three-inches tall and lanky, my pants had to be altered. One day while in the store, I tried on a pair of trousers. The clerk had to measure the inseam because one of my legs is slightly longer than the other. While he was measuring the inseam, to my horror, his hands touched my private parts. This was very disturbing to me. After they were altered, I never returned to Baldwin's. I had been violated. I told my friends, and they boycotted the store.

When I was a boy, *Amos and Andy* and other minstrel shows denigrated colored people. Another means of stereotyping blacks was the face of "Aunt Jemima," who epitomized the black female house servant: plump, smiling, wearing a bandana, and having overly large eyes and lips. I shall never forget that in 1940 when *Gone with the Wind* was released in Hollywood (a 3.5-hour movie with an intermission), Hattie McDaniels played the housemaid who took care of Miss Scarlet and her family. Nothing in the movie *Gone with the Wind* depicts blacks as human beings—only servants. This is what I observed during my formative and teenage years.

There was one eccentric lady in town that brought all the latest gossip to the store. While having her refreshments, she spoke about T.G., the newly married wife of a prominent family in town. She muttered, "This family is supposed to be at the top of the social ladder. The parents used to be chauffeured to Florida in the winter." One day, she loudly proclaimed that the son had "disappointed the parents by marrying a woman who used to sit on an orange crate and fix hair." He had married below his status as a lawyer in town. Another day she talked about her black maid, who had worked for her many years. The young woman was dark-skinned and was arrested for a domestic dispute one evening. She was sentenced to a year in jail. Ten months later, she delivered a lily-white baby.

Before I quit working at the store, I had gotten to know the prominent people in town by name (not personally): people who had money such as tobacco barons, insurance brokers, bankers, pharmacists, doctors, businessmen and women. It was an education just working there and being an invisible boy. I kept my mouth shut, listened, and learned. Some of the people I encountered still have children and grandchildren in Prince Edward County.

Another scandal occurred when I was in tenth-grade in high school: I had a female classmate who was dating the minister's son. In the spring time, they would go over to the river and find a place to have sex. This was a hush-hush matter. Eventually, she became pregnant and married the boy who was a senior at the time. That was the talk of the town.

In those days, we were told about reefers (marijuana cigarettes), and porn consisting of a little 3"x 5" inch book that had line drawings of people having sex. All the guys would flock to get a peek and pass it along. When I was a teenager, my father talked to us about VD, condoms, and sexually transmitted diseases. He scared the life out of us with his vivid descriptions. I never to this day understood why condoms were called "merry widows," a term that now is obsolete.

The last story I remember is the incident in which a prominent builder had a custom-made home with a wife and three children. His wife took the children to Virginia Beach for a weekend and came home to find a black woman in her bed with her husband. Later, there was a mixed child from this union. There are very few new things in life—history tends to repeat itself.

BALTIMORE

During the late 30s and early 40s, four of my brothers headed north to Baltimore to find work at Bethlehem Steel Company in Sparrows Point, Maryland. They lived in a rooming house with a cousin, Bill Ford, and his wife Mary.

 I would often visit my older brothers in Baltimore during the summer school breaks. They took good care of me. Time was always found to take me to parks, museums, and theaters. They made sure I was well-dressed from head to toe, and I did not need anything for college. While in Baltimore, I met many peers my age. Some spoke Spanish, so I resented the fact that Moton did not offer Spanish for us to learn.

In Baltimore, there were two theatres, the Regent and the Royal, both on Pennsylvania Avenue. I attended matinees that included news, cartoons, and a movie followed by a well-known band. It was here that I was introduced to some of the greatest popular music artists in the world. I will never forget the sounds of The Duke of Ellington, The Count of Basie, and The Earl of Hines bands. Their jazz orchestras were always accompanied by singers like Ella Fitzgerald, Sarah Vaughn, Lil Green, and Billy Holiday. They took me into another world. Each band had its own unique qualities. The audience would respond with rapture and would remain on its feet, applauding for minutes after every performance.

I had a cousin named William Ford who played with Cootie Williams. In those days, he was not permitted to stay in white hotels or lodges. Looking back, it was very difficult for these talented and bright musicians to make a living. The big white jazz bands visited Longwood and Hampden Sydney Colleges, so I developed an appreciation for the music of Tommy Dorsey, Glenn Miller, Stan Kenton, and others.

In high school, we played on our record player songs like "Tuxedo Junction," "In the Mood," "Take the A Train," "White Christmas," "Straighten Up and Fly Right," and "One O'Clock Jump." Sometimes we had enough time to dance a few minutes, and make small talk, as teenagers do, before returning to classes. Artists recorded their music on vinyl records: 33 1/3, 45 and 78 revolutions per minute. It cost five cents to play one record.

Before jukeboxes, my father bought us an RCA Victrola. It had an arm with a crank that had to be wound up to play music. We placed the record on the turn table, lifted the needle, placed it on the edge of the record, and then listened. Occasionally, if it was too tightly wound, the machine would break. The needle had to be frequently replaced. After prolonged use, it would scratch the record.

I am still a big band era fan. It's the music that defined my youth. Listening to the orchestras taught me how to recognize tones and appreciate the various solo instruments.

During those days, jazz and bebop became very popular, and there was more improvisation, creativity, and exploring than there is today. I learned to appreciate the music of the thirties and forties. In the 50s, I was in the Army and had no time to tune in. In the 60s, I was in graduate school where music and the new wave of stars had no meaning for me. I had no time to devote to it. My studies came first!

MEMORIES OF MOTON

In the summer of 2008, three of my classmates, whom I graduated with in 1944, decided to meet in Farmville and reminisce about our school days. We talked about our teachers and how they gave 100% to help us learn. They poured into us all their talent to help us achieve. They knew that "we were the future generation" and that we had to be well-educated to succeed. I still remember Mrs. Altona Trent Johns, wife of Rev. Vernon Johns (civil rights activist and gifted preacher), who taught music. She also taught English and directed the chorus. Once a week she required us to assemble in the auditorium with our song books and sing from *Finlandia, Cavalleria Rusticana, Tannhauser*, and other great works. I only realize today what she had exposed us to. High schools in those days used to have competitions in choral singing, and our school always participated. Superintendent of Schools T. J. McIllwaine would invite his white friends to our school to hear Mrs. Johns play the baby grand piano. She was a master of music and the author of several books. Each time I hear classical music today, I think of her.

At the Styles Family Reunion in 2016, we reflected on the trials and tribulations we faced before *Brown v. Board of Education* and the strike. One of my classmates, Mrs. Hilda Johnson Cosby from Hampden Sydney, Virginia, earned a degree in Home Economics from St. Paul's College in

Lawrenceville, Virginia, and worked as a teacher and county official for Henrico County, Virginia. She retired as an assistant to a banker and was curator of the Museum in Memory of Virginia E. Randolph in Glen Allen, Virginia, until her health began to fail in 2014. Sadly, my friend Hilda just died on July 10, 2018. I will miss her.

Mrs. Mary Frances Bell Watkins now lives in Kenbridge, Virginia, and spoke about having to walk a great distance in the rain and snow to catch a bus. She was married to the late Rev. Haywood Watkins, a graduate of the Moton Class of 1941. She lived in the Green Bay area of PEC and had to ride a small school bus that everyday carried fifteen students to Moton. These children had to awaken at 6:00 a.m. to be bussed for over 20 miles to arrive for 8:30 a.m. classes every morning. It cost $1.25 a week to take the bus. On more than one day the bus broke down, and she would have to walk about fifteen miles to get to school. She and others would get up in the dark on mornings and not get home until after dark. Most people have no idea how difficult it was for her and others to do this every day. I lived in Farmville and had to walk about a mile to the school.

One of the high school students I taught turned out to be one of the leaders of the students who went on strike in 1951. The Rev. Samuel Williams, Jr., is now a minister at Levi Baptist church, not far from his home in Farmville. We have kept in touch over the years, and he told me how he was jailed for four days because he was involved in the demonstrations to reopen the public schools in PEC between 1959 and 1964. In 1963, the police almost put him and others in the PEC jail but didn't because they were afraid that a riot might ensue. Instead, he and others were placed in the nearby Lunenburg County jail but were shortly bailed out by Rev. Leslie Francis Griffin.

Dr. Nathan Miller, a prominent dentist and Deacon of First Baptist church, was a champion of education for us and was generous with financial support of our cause. His wife also taught at Moton. During the summer of 1963, he and some young ministers were leaders in the demonstrations against the closing of the schools in PEC. He had been a student in my biology class at Moton in 1949 and was very loquacious and vocal. I observed leadership qualities in him at the time.

In 1963, these demonstrations occurred in many places I had worked or shopped in the 1940s. Most occurred downtown on Main Street. Protesters tried to gain access to the old Echo Theater, the College Shoppe restaurant, and Chappell's Fountain and Bookstore. They encountered locked doors and resistance from white churches and store owners, even at Chappell's where I had worked for four years while I attended Moton from 1941 to 1944. Sammy Williams told me that an attempt was made to enter the Farmville Methodist Church (an all-white church across from Longwood College) and Farmville Baptist Church (also all-white), but the protesters were turned away. Their ushers instead pointed them toward my church—First Baptist Church of Farmville (all black)—but Sammy and some young ministers ignored them and decided to go to the Farmville Baptist Church anyway. Their ushers said, "You people are not coming in here," so the feisty and fearless Sammy Williams decided to have church on the steps of the Farmville Baptist Church. He lead his group in prayer and in the singing of several civil rights songs including "Let Us Break Bread Together," and "We Shall Overcome." Sammy Williams published a book, *Exile E*, that addressed the contributions of black churches to the protests against the school closings in Prince Edward County from 1959 through 1964. He sent me an autographed copy of it on March 30th, 2012, with the following acknowledgement:

> *"For the Styles': Master teachers and committed parents and community members."*

*"Brother Styles, an integral part of my rearing our children
was to convey to them and their children that which you so
often shared with us in biology class: "Don't play the game
of catch you—play the game of keep up!" And "coming to
class without paper and pencil is like going hunting without
a gun." Also, your biology class caused me to develop an
interest in science and its contributions to religion and to
my Christian ministry, specifically and especially in the
areas of anthropology, astronomy, and archeology. Stay
strong and fight onward! God bless! Love you."*

While all the protests were occurring, I was working my way through
NYU's Graduate School of Arts and Sciences. Even though I had no time
to join them on the front lines, I did have the opportunity to go and participate in the famous August 28, 1963, Jobs and Freedom March where Martin Luther King spoke in Washington, D.C. I was fortunate and blessed to
hear his "I Have a Dream" speech live and in person. Words can't describe
what an experience that was! The next day I returned to my job and studies
at NYU.

FARMVILLE - MY HOMETOWN

Farmville is the county seat for Prince Edward County. In my day, it was a small town that had furniture stores, department stores, churches, and many streets. Main Street was the hub of town where all the action took place. The county courthouse was located there. People from all over the surrounding counties went to Main Street to sell products, buy clothes, shoes, and furniture, and to meet friends and attend movies.

I was constantly impressed by the roles colored people played in Farmville. Our mailman was colored, and three restaurants, two gas stations, several barber shops, three churches, two dry cleaning establishments, two funeral homes, and a pool room were owned by coloreds. Many owned cars, property, houses of ill repute, and bootleg liquor joints, too. We also had several social clubs like The Elks, The Masons, Noblesse Oblige, and the Martha E. Forrester Council of Colored Women, which recognized the need for educational, social, and civic activities to uplift our community. Its motto was "Lifting as We Climb," and its goals were:

- To furnish systematic help for the uplift of Negroes in our community.
- To improve educational advantages for the Negroes of the community.
- To secure harmony of action and cooperation among people of Farmville.

- To improve the home life, the morals, and the civic life of our people.
- To minister to the less fortunate.

I knew four of the officers in the organization. They felt that their immediate priority was addressing the educational needs of our children. The areas of deepest concern were providing adequate building facilities, lengthening the school term, providing bus transportation, and securing a four-year accredited high school. The council worked zealously to raise money for building improvements and for lengthening the school year to eight months.

In 1996, The Martha E. Forrester Council of Women committed to buying Moton H.S. from the county for $300,000. The building is now on the National Registry of Historical Places. Today, all but one of the tar paper shacks are gone (the only one left is part of a display), and my old high school building where I studied and then returned to as a teacher has been converted to a civil rights museum.

It is no secret that the tireless dedication and hard work of these black women was crucial to the improvement of educational opportunities available to black students in Farmville. Their work also catalyzed support for "The Strike," which I will explain in forthcoming chapters.

ROLE MODELS

Farmville was known basically as a farm town. Many people, especially the Negroes (as we were called back then), worked in the fields on farms for a living. Others were employed at menial jobs by Longwood College. Many washed clothes and were cooks and nannies.

Who were my role models in town? First and foremost, my father was my role model. Pa was a strong, thoughtful, no-nonsense guy. He was a very likable, peaceful man who did not confront people but did not take any "crap" from anyone who disrespected him or any member of his family. Everyone knew not to "mess with Peter Styles." He was not aggressive, but he was a quick responder. He was exceedingly observant, tolerant, patient, kind, caring, a good provider, and someone who possessed good judgment of people's characters. One could never figure out what he was thinking. He also liked to read the *Farmville Herald* and listen to the radio when time permitted.

Other role models that left a lasting impression upon me were the Rev. Dr. Vernon Johns, Baptist preacher, civil rights activist, farmer, orator, and father of six children. He and his wife, Altona, had three boys and three girls.

Born in Darlington Heights, Prince Edward County, Rev. Johns was a brilliant thinker who at the age of 10 taught himself Latin, Greek, German, and Hebrew. Early in his career, he delivered fiery sermons against "separate but not equal" public facilities, criticizing both blacks and whites alike for failing to work in earnest for complete equality for blacks. His preaching genius and his adamant fight for social justice gained him much respect in the black community. He would come home to Farmville and speak in a loud voice about why blacks should support each other economically and spiritually. He was a mentor to many budding black ministers. He stressed racial pride and social justice, influenced many future civil rights leaders, and became pastor of Dexter Avenue Baptist Church in Montgomery, Alabama, where Dr. Martin Luther King later preached. His wife taught music and English at Moton High School. When I was a student at Moton High School, I knew all of his children, and I was in touch with his youngest surviving son, John Johns, until his death on August 26th, 2016. John Johns and his wife Elizabeth were family friends and attended many of the Styles Family reunions. When Pastor Vernon Johns preached, one could hear him denouncing and demonizing the white man from blocks away. Despite his critical rhetoric, I don't think he ever received any threats from the white power structure in town.

LONGWOOD UNIVERSITY AND EMINENT DOMAIN

From 1959-1964, the public schools were shut down in PEC as local officials resisted desegregation orders. Our elementary school was across the
street from the Longwood University (formerly Farmville State Teachers
College) Campus. I don't think that the administrators at Longwood or
Hampden-Sydney, a Presbyterian College, resisted actively the history un-
folding at their doorsteps, but many students have countless tales to tell
about the worry and stress they endured while their elementary schools
were closed.

My home was located only a few blocks from Longwood College,
where Blacks were forced from their homes so that it could expand its campus. My sister's home on Ely Street and my father's home on Race Street
were affected by the county's claim of eminent domain. Longwood's ex-
pansion also negatively affected black neighborhoods comprised mainly
of elderly individuals on fixed incomes. This mandatory displacement of
families created a panic, and caused many elderly residents to find a new
place to live, which was confusing and frightening for them.

My family's home was purchased for the lowest price on the market.
We had a lovely home with an apple tree and plum tree, and many children played in our backyard, especially during the summer. We have fond

memories of growing up there with my father, step-mother, sisters, brothers, and their children. We had wonderful family gatherings on Race Street, but because our house was bought by Longwood College, the place where our memories were formed was taken away from us and other black land owners.

MARTHA E. FORRESTER COUNCIL OF COLORED WOMEN

The Martha E. Forrester Council of Colored Women was founded in 1920 by Martha E. Forrester, a public school teacher in Richmond, and other black women whom she knew. This group of pioneering women and community leaders catalyzed the construction of Moton High School in 1939.

In 1969, the council assumed the responsibility of developing the old Moton H.S. into a civil rights museum. In 1995, the school board transferred the property back to the county supervisors who then agreed to sell the building to the Martha E. Forrester Council for $300,000. The 75th anniversary of the Martha E. Forrester Council of Colored Women was celebrated on Sunday, April 13th, 1995. There were sixteen charter members including Mrs. Forrester herself. Her daughter, Mrs. Jeannette Clark (my sixth-grade teacher), Mrs. Maida V. McKnight, president of the Noblesse Oblige Club, and my niece, Barbara Dixon, and my stepmother, Carroll Styles, were amongst other members of the club. At this 75th anniversary celebration, tributes were paid to Rev. Vernon Johns, preacher and civil rights activist and uncle of Barbara Johns. Moreover, citizens and civic leaders of Farmville gathered on December 10th, 2017, for the dedication of the new Barbara Rose Johns Farmville-Prince Edward Library. This event was the community's recognition of the significant contribution Barbara Rose Johns made to make freedom and justice for all a reality rather than just an ideal. I have visited this library as well as the Moton Museum several times over the years. In 1998, after many years of keeping it open and viable, the Moton School was added to the National Historic Landmark Registry. I have visited the museum several times over the years. The museum focuses on the years from 1951 until the present—events prior to 1951 are not covered.

ROBERT R. MOTON MUSEUM

In April 2013, the $5.5 million Robert R. Moton Museum opened with six galleries and exhibits that document and reflect the thirteen-year struggle to achieve equal educational opportunities for blacks in PEC. In July 2015, the Moton Museum and Longwood University finalized an affiliation in perpetuity in which Longwood would provide operational, financial, and administrative support for the museum. The Museum has 501(c)(3)-status and will continue to have an independent status as a non-profit organization. Looking back, I wonder where Longwood and Hampden Sydney Colleges were during the time the struggle was going on. Why didn't they and other civic organizations (i.e., churches, clubs, and businesses) do more to help the struggle? It was lack of education by these members of the community and deep rooted racism, I suspect. Moreover, an "us versus them" mindset was part of the DNA of many PEC citizens, and unfortunately, their ingrained negative feelings towards blacks were present back then, and have not gone away yet. White privilege and bigotry still raises its head today in Farmville.

It will be interesting to see how the affiliation of Longwood and the museum plays out. Will blacks really have a seat at the table? Or, will they go back to the days when they were the cooks, maids, lawn keepers, and janitors? My hope is that many of the children and grandchildren of people who were subjugated in the past will be in positions of power in the future. Will they be able to effect improvements in race relations in PEC? Keep your eyes open, because only time will tell.

VIRGINIA UNION UNIVERSITY

VUU is the result of the fusion of the Richmond Theological Seminary for Freed Men and the Wayland Seminary in Washington, D.C., in 1899. These two institutions were established in 1865 by the American Baptist Society. At this time, VUU was all male. In 1932, Hartshorn Memorial College, established in 1883 for the education of young, Negro women, was united with Virginia Union University to make it coeducational.

After the World's Fair ended in New York in 1942, the Belgian Friendship Building on display there was donated to VUU. But, money had to be raised to dismantle and transport it from Flushing, NY, and then reconstruct it on the VUU campus in Richmond, Virginia. Eventually, it was moved but was never functional while I was a student at VUU.

While I attended VUU, I was a biology major and took part in the choir, theater group, and student government. In fact, I played a role in the drama club's performance of Emily Bronte's *Wuthering Heights*, directed by a professor who also worked for theaters on Broadway. Beyond these activities, there were not many other electives or other opportunities in art or music. VUU offered the minimum number of courses to be classified as a liberal arts college. We had approximately forty full-time teachers, four administrators, and a total enrollment of 600. There were

80 in our graduating class, and I was elected president of the junior and senior classes.

Virginia Union was also a Christian school—we had to attend chapel three times per week—and were urged to go to church every Sunday. The University also had a seminary graduate program that prepared students to pursue Christian ministry. There was an aura of spirituality on the campus because of the number of divinity students enrolled.

Mrs. Ruby Dahlia Moon Brinkley taught Latin my first year there. She was a force to be reckoned with. When we entered her classroom, she would be standing by an open window, praying. She would introduce herself and say to the class, "Ruby stands for precious stone. Dahlias stands for flowers. Moon for search light, and Brinkley stands alone." She said it with such conviction that I never forgot her. Her husband was on the faculty of the Theology Department, and she prayed for us to get a good education and succeed because she knew we represented the future. She was a very powerful woman.

At VUU, there were four fraternities and four sororities, and interscholastic football, basketball, and tennis teams. I pledged Alpha Phi Alpha Fraternity and was initiated on May 6th, 1946. It was the first black college fraternity in the nation, founded in 1904 at Cornell University, with successive chapters at Howard University, and VUU, respectively. I was greatly influenced by the brotherhood and fellowship within the Alphas. In fact, today I belong to a graduate chapter in the Capital District. The Alphas are known as a service organization with love for all mankind. We have many outstanding members and contribute to many social and educational activities in the community.

During my years at VUU, "panty raids" were popular. Even though VUU was very strict, the boys had a bit more freedom than the women did.

At night, the members of AΦA would stand outside the girls' dormitory and serenade them for an hour or so. The young ladies would stand at their windows, wave their panties, and scream with delight. How the panty raids took place in such a strict environment still remains a mystery to me!

I had saved five hundred dollars for my first-year tuition at VUU, and traveled from Farmville to Richmond in the back of a Greyhound bus. When I arrived in Richmond, I took a cab to the campus. I reported to Kingsley Hall, a male dormitory where upperclassmen looked us over and checked us out. I was finally assigned to a room with two other fellows. The lighting was poor, the floors splintered, and the beds infested with bedbugs. It was not the most comfortable place to be, but I did not want to go back home. During the week, an exterminator would come and spray the frame of the bed and mattress. I could smell the odor of an insecticide for days. It was a disgustingly pungent odor that made you feel sick when in your dorm room and if you were trying to study there. You had to keep the windows open.

It was the fall of 1944, and WWII was still being waged. Food was scarce, and there was rationing. We had a dietician named Miss Moss, who oversaw food services. She stood behind the cafeteria line and monitored every plate. We had three meals a day, except for Sundays. On Sundays, there were only two, breakfast and lunch. We had a sandwich and a piece of fruit for supper.

During my first semester, I took Economics 101 under Professor Gordon Blaine Hancock, Pastor of Moore Street Baptist Church in Richmond. He was a leading spokesman for African American equality in the generation before the civil rights movement. He co-founded the Richmond Urban League and wrote newspaper columns for the *African American Associated Press*, advising blacks how to get by in tough times while still taking a stand against the segregation movement. During the Great Depression, he cautioned black workers to hold on to their jobs when possible yet urged us never to forget the economic, educational, and political issues that affected the entire black community. He also taught sociology and linked education to activism, requiring students to perform community service.

African Americans were having such a hard time after WWII that, according to Hancock, "When most blacks get to a point in life that they can have a home and enjoy a good quality of life, they usually die. They never get a chance to enjoy it." That statement was prophetic, as I am now ninety-one years of age and understand what he meant. The knowledge I received in Hancock's economics class has always stayed with me until today.

As I look back at my childhood and college friends, his pronouncement was true. Many blacks during my generation had to work long, hard, and diligently to get married and support a family. Our families had nothing to pass along to us such as money, homes, furniture or an inheritance. We had to earn everything that we have today. The hours were long, the boss was mean, and the environment was not always hospitable. We persevered, and somehow, with divine guidance, we were able to accomplish something. Not only have many of us been able to move upward but are now in a place to make sure our children and grandchildren get the best possible education available. One of the things I am most proud of is that both of our children were able to get a fine education at Princeton University.

ALPHA PHI ALPHA FRATERNITY

Alpha Phi Alpha Fraternity was the first black intercollegiate Greek-lettered fraternity. I was initiated into the Gamma Chapter at Virginia Union University. I have been a member for seventy years and am still active in Beta Pi Lambda subchapter located in Albany, NY. The fraternity evolved from a collection of African-American males who shared a lot in common into mostly a service organization that provided members with leadership opportunities during the Great Depression, both World Wars, and the Civil Rights Movement. Some of the notable members of Alpha Phi Alpha included Vernon Johns, Martin Luther King, Jr., Jesse Owens, Lionel Richie, and Maynard Jackson. The Pi Pi Chapter was founded at Union College in 1983, and my friend and colleague Dr. George Smith, Ph.D., was the catalyst and advisor for the group. The thirtieth Anniversary Gala was held on May 30th, 2013, at the college during Reunion Weekend.

Brother George Smith, a cell biology professor at Union College, and I, amongst other brothers, were honored at this event. There were fifty brothers who returned for fellowship, connection, communication, socialization, and networking: about 150 altogether. Later that year, we established an endowed internship to support college students interested in community service. The award was named after Mohammed A. Omar, a brother of Pi Pi chapter, who died in a tragic boating accident during the summer of 1993.

Many student members of Pi Pi Chapter have distinguished themselves in many fields. Two have become orthopedic surgeons: Dr. Anthony B. Ndu graduated from Yale, and Dr. Kirk Campbell from New York University. Brother Solomon Jenkins III, engineer, worked for GE in Schenectady for 33 years. Jay Harris was an ESPN Sports Center anchor, and part of their Emmy-winning efforts in 2004 and 2005. Robert Jay "Bubba Thrice" Koonce was an outstanding football player at Union from 1982 until 1985. He earned his Master's Degree in Educational Administration at the University of Michigan and worked in the Office of Admissions and Athletic Department at several colleges and universities. At our 2013 Anniversary Gala, a poignant tribute was paid to our late brother Koonce and his family by Union College football coach John Audino.

Alpha Phi Alpha's historical purpose was to provide an academic and social support group for all minority students who encountered social and academic racial prejudice. Like most black fraternities and sororities at historically black colleges and universities, membership is based upon scholarship, and not economic or family status. Most college students in those days were the first members of their families to pursue a college degree. The Alpha Preamble states:

> *To promote a more perfect union among college men; to aid and insist upon the personal progress of its members; to further brotherly love and fraternal spirit within the organization; to discountenance evil; to destroy all prejudices; and to preserve the sanctity of the home, the personification of virtue, and the chastity of women.*

The members of this fraternity continue a legacy of distinctive service to all. In 2017, Dr. Marshall Jones, a leading, globally recognized, mechanical engineer, and fellow Alpha brother was inducted into the National Inventors Hall of Fame for his pioneering work on industrial lasers. While working at General Electric, he was awarded 50 U.S. and 31 foreign patents.

MOTON HIGH — SCIENCE TEACHER

In the fall of 1944, I matriculated at Virginia Union University in Richmond, Virginia, earning a B.S. in Biology in May 1948. Subsequently, I was offered my first teaching job at Moton High School. I accepted it and was assigned to teach science courses. The high school was named after Robert Russa Moton, a noted educator from neighboring Amelia County. The school was built in 1939 to accommodate 180 students. It had eight classrooms, two bathrooms, an auditorium that held approximately 300 students, and a principal's office. All classes had to pass through the auditorium to get from one room to another. The auditorium had a baby grand piano and removable seats that could be taken up and replaced when needed. It was used for convocations, school choir, drama club, and study hall. The library had some books, however, the science equipment was outdated and often did not function.

We did not have a cafeteria, gymnasium, teacher's restrooms, or any facilities for physical education: There was no basketball court, swimming pool, or anything to help develop the body.

During the two years I was there, due to overcrowding, three plywood tar shack buildings were constructed to accommodate the students. These shacks had pot belly stoves that had to be fired up all day to keep us warm.

Some courses were even taught in an immobile school bus. The conditions were dire. I recall that back in the late 1930's, money was appropriated for public schools in Prince Edward County. Most of these funds ended up at the white Farmville High School, where the physical plant and offerings were far superior. It was located on First Avenue, and was a huge two-story brick building on approximately two acres of manicured lawns. It's a wonder that geniuses were not produced. The white students did not want for anything, yet we blacks wanted for everything. It's odd how some people still blame blacks for their lack of education and for being in trouble with the law all the time when for most of America's history they had subpar educational opportunities at best.

When someone has been denied an opportunity for an education and the system discourages that person from obtaining one, who is to blame for crime and not being prepared for the work force? All black people are not dumb—we just need an opportunity to pursue a better quality of life. However, even after one gets an education, barriers are in place to keep us from moving forward. This is not only true for blacks in the military and academia but for other races as well. It is the supervisor's mindset: the belief that one is inherently superior to another and need not account for his or her behavior towards others. Although the struggle against the systemic racial injustice that impacted me in my lifetime continues, much has been accomplished, and I am confident that the barriers to educational opportunity will continue to fall.

ARMY - KOREAN CONFLICT

I was inducted into the U.S. Army in October 1950 at Fort Meade, Maryland. We spent about a week acclimating ourselves to this new environment before being shipped to Fort Jackson, South Carolina (close to Columbia, SC), for basic training. Before I left, many people admonished me not to go into the city of Colombia because of racial incidents that had been occurring there. Due to the warning and tension, I stayed on the base throughout my training.

Once there, we were given a foot locker, a wall locker, a rifle, and uniforms to be prepared for winter. I was a "ninety-nine-pound weakling" when I went into the Army, but that changed after two weeks. Why? Our sergeant in charge was a former marine, and he was as tough as whit leather—the skin of animals tanned with alum or salt—and as strong as a horse. Having a former marine sergeant lead my squad, it did not take me long to realize that I needed to be strong and ready to protect our country. I quickly learned that the training was designed to instill in us the "to kill or be killed" mindset as we prepared for war.

I completed the requirements of basic training: I learned how to shoot a .45 side arm pistol, machine gun, M-1 rifle, bazooka, and to wield a bayonet and throw grenades. For me, it was a new experience, and I quickly realized that we trainees were not playing fiddlesticks. It was the real deal. I appreciated the leader because he was thorough and did not take any slack from anyone. After going through basic, we boys on the field were now the men who were prepared to face the enemy in battle.

I further appreciated my sergeant because he made sure we learned how to take care of ourselves and our buddies. He prepared us to go to the Korean War. He taught us the critical importance of adherence to the chain of command structure, how to listen and follow orders, and how to keep our M1 rifles as clean as a whistle and as neat as a pin. He was a no-nonsense guy. If someone in our barracks messed up, he would awaken us and say, "Be ready for a five-mile run before breakfast." After training was over, I felt confident that I could take care of business if called upon. The thing I really enjoyed most were the parades. On Saturdays, we had to march in gear in front of the generals and put our best feet forward.

When we completed our basic training, we were given a two-week leave. Following our leave, my buddies and I returned to the base and soon learned that our battalion was shipping off to Korea. It was early in the spring of 1951, and things were heating up in the Korean Conflict. I, along with hundreds of soldiers with all of our worldly possessions in a duffel bag and rifle in hand, boarded the ship to face the unknown.

Aboard the ship, the sleeping quarters were tight the air was stale. Our quarters were only yards away from the mess hall, and once I entered the mess hall, I could smell a terrible odor that always made me nauseous. I never did get used to it—we all had to stand up for our meals and endure it. Later, I found out the smell was an insecticide to help control the roaches. It was so pungent that I can still smell it now. On another note, some days we would run into Pacific storms, and the ship would roll, pitch, and sway from side to side and up and down. The deck was slippery, and one had to hold on for dear life to keep from being swept overboard.

Some nights when the weather was calm and the temperature right, I slept on the deck. I recall on one moonlit evening when the ocean near our ship was aglow. My training as a biologist made me aware that the light was due the presence of beautiful phosphorescent protozoans swarming on top of the water. They glowed like yellow-bellied fireflies. It was as if they had guided and lit our path across the Pacific to Yokohama.

YOKOHAMA TO TOKYO

After disembarking from the ship, our battalion was bussed to a camp in Yokohama. No one knew what was going to happen. Because I had a bachelor's of science degree in biology, I was summoned one day to speak to a captain. He asked me about my college degree and asked me if I wanted to go to Korea. I looked him in his eyes and said, "Captain, I am better prepared to handle a microscope than a rifle," and later that day, a miracle happened.

We were scheduled to take a train from Yokohama to Southern Japan to board a ship that would take us to the war zone. There must have been more than 500 soldiers in line with their rifles and duffel bags, armed with fear about what was going to happen next. As my fellow comrades and I were lined up, each person's last name was yelled over a loudspeaker, and then they boarded the train. When they got to my name, a sergeant said in a loud booming voice, "STYLES, STEP ASIDE." I didn't know why this happened, but I was sent back to the processing camp. I did not know what was going to happen to me. Three days later, I received my orders to join the Occupation Forces in Tokyo. My duty was to be stationed at the 406th, the Medical General Laboratory in the Department of Medical Zoology.

The U.S. Army Medical Corp and Centers for Disease Control are constantly monitoring all kinds of diseases. Citizens at home and servicemen abroad are affected by these infections. It is vital to our mission and for our ability to effectively wage war that our troops and military personnel be healthy and wary of communicable diseases. The military has many ways to fight a war on the ground, in the air, and at sea. Most people never think about the importance of the medical support: soldiers can't fight if they are ill and sick. I was both lucky and proud to be able to use my undergraduate training in service to my country.

406th MEDICAL GENERAL LABORATORY

The 406th Medical General Laboratory was a stand-alone unit that served as the place to train and teach Army doctors and health care workers about the exotic diseases most American doctors had not seen and only read about in textbooks. It also provided the major laboratory for FECOM's (Far East Command) specialized research on communicable parasitic diseases and testing of illegal drugs. Army doctors and medical personnel had to spend at least six weeks there before they were assigned to Korea and the Far East.

The laboratory was a large four-story building that spanned a half block. Personnel stationed there studied viral infections with cutaneous lesions, enteroviral infections, febrile viral infections, encephalitis, and hemorrhagic fevers. There was also a department of bacteriology whose members had expertise in fungal, protozoan, and helminth infections, entomology, and vector transmissible diseases. It was the premier place for a young biologist to be stationed when it came to taking care of our military and civilian employees in the Far East.

Also at the 406th was Colonel George W. Hunter III, a parasitologist and educator with the U.S. Army Sanitary Corps and Army Medical School, who was best known for his work in *schistosomiasis* (snail fever) control. He was a member of the faculty of the Tropical Military Medicine Course, which expanded in 1942 from 23 to 200 students, at the Army Medical School. In 1945, he suggested offering his course as the basis of a textbook that was later published as the *Manual of Tropical Medicine,* subsequent editions of which became the standard reference in the field. The United States forces occupying Japan required food handlers to be free of parasites, and Hunter fielded a mobile laboratory outfitted in railroad cars that tested nearly nineteen thousand Japanese.

In 1949, researchers found 93.2 percent of those tested were infected with some form of intestinal parasite. To investigate these parasites, we were staffed with four commissioned officers, three DAC (Department of Army Civilians), and fifteen Japanese nationals. Working in Hunter's laboratory inspired me to seek an advanced degree in parasitology when I was discharged from the Army. In his laboratory, I was trained to become an expert diagnostician of intestinal and blood parasites, and felt honored when he selected me to teach laboratory diagnosis for two weeks at the Osaka Army Hospital. I felt that I had truly arrived to be given this responsibility, and to this day, I thank him for granting me this opportunity. Hunter and his American and Japanese colleagues were able to investigate and initiate efforts that eventually led to the virtual eradication of snail fever from Japan. One city in Japan later erected a statue honoring him for his success in eliminating it from a district in their area.

When I arrived at the 406th, I was assigned to work with Dr. Lin, a brilliant doctor from Okinawa. He was an expert in his field and the chief diagnostician for people who became infected with malaria, dysentery, and other intestinal infections. I worked beside him the entire time I was there. He was gracious enough to teach me all that he knew for me to become an expert in this area. The other responsibility of the 406th was to provide fresh whole blood to soldiers in Korea and wherever it was needed to support combat divisions and battalions during periods of heavy fighting. Medical officers in Korea knew that blood transfusions for the injured could save the lives of wounded combatants.

FINANCE BUILDING-TOKYO

I was one of many soldiers quartered in the Tokyo finance building where soldiers were housed for sleeping. The finance building was huge and guarded twenty-four hours per day by military police. There, I met a soldier named Quinones, a Mexican who worked in another department of the 406th. He was a compassionate person, and one Sunday, with his Bible in hand, asked me to accompany him to Tokyo General Hospital where wounded soldiers from Korea were sent to be treated for gunshot wounds, frostbite, and other injuries.

We took a bus to the hospital, and arrived at 11:00 a.m. We went to a ward where they cared for new patients arriving from the front lines. As we walked through the ward, he would often stop and pray for and with the many injured soldiers. Suddenly, I heard someone call me name: "Twitty?" I turned around and saw two of my buddies from basic training in South Carolina. They were waiting to be discharged and return by train to fight on the frontlines in Korea. While they waited, I recall how glad I was to see them. During our brief visit, they shared horrific stories of many friends killed or maimed in battle, and told of the soldiers with self-inflicted wounds to avoid the front lines. I recall my sadness as I thought about my squad buddies from Fort Jackson returning to the fury and danger of battle.

They asked me to send them cartons of cigarettes and other personal items. I often thought about how easy it could have been me lying in a hospital bed, and me returning to the front lines of the warzone. I was very lucky.

After a long day at the hospital, we walked back to the 406th and passed the Japanese Imperial Palace surrounded by a water-filled moat. In the winter, it was frozen, but in the early spring, the warmer temperatures melted the moat's ice cover, and we could see dead bodies floating on the surface of the water—a sight I will never forget.

Another thing that I will never forget is when one day I was not feeling well, I went to my quarters to sleep. I saw four men come in with a soldier. The four demanded him to open his locker. I pretended that I was sleeping and peeped out of the corner of my left eye. I watched as the men removed a wide-brimmed ladies hat, a long green evening gown, high-heeled shoes, and a locker full of ladies' things. I was shocked. Apparently, that weekend, the soldier whose locker was searched had attended a same-sex marriage in Yokohama.

The Criminal Investigation Division (CID) took into custody the soldier who was over six feet tall and weighed around 180 pounds. He did not say anything to the officers. Later, I learned that he was the son of a Columbia University professor and was a bridesmaid at one of his friend's weddings in Yokohama. When I look back, I didn't know anything about same-sex marriages. I was shocked. In the 50s, same-sex marriages were not heard of.

While in Tokyo, I spent time marveling at the Japanese culture. It was new and so different from anything I had experienced while growing up in Farmville. I went to the Kabuki Theater, Shinto shrines, hot baths and spas, climbed Mount Fujiyama and saw a production of Puccini's *Madame Butterfly*. It was interesting to note that in the third act of the opera, when Pinkerton brings his American wife to take his son back to America, she was depicted as a pale, nappy-haired, washed-out blonde. She was not depicted as the typical high-class American lady that I saw at a theater in Richmond when I was a student. The Japanese production was so different, and reminded me of one day while walking down an avenue in Tokyo I noticed a Japanese girl with blonde hair. What a sight to behold!

My Japanese co-workers taught me Japanese, but there was a cold war with Russia at the time, and Russia was rattling its sword. I decided to go to the Armed Forces Language School and take Russian. I satisfactorily completed introductory Russian but never used it. I did not know it at the time, but my experiences at the 406th would inspire me to pursue a career in parasitology.

REST AND RECUPERATION (R AND R)

In early 1951, the Army began a program to raise sagging morale. "R and R" leaves were available to generals and GIs alike. They helped us to endure the everyday loneliness, exhaustion, and dangers that soldiers face, especially those soldiers that served on the front lines in Korea. War-exhausted men looked forward to a week-long holiday in Japan.

Tokyo, with its bright lights and exotic culture, was dazzling. Clubs for officers, noncoms, and enlisted men provided entertainment ranging from familiar American jazz and pop tunes to Japanese food, great beer, and polite, exotic girls. GIs on leave had the opportunity to meet American girls serving as military nurses or as civilians with support roles in occupied Japan.

The Japanese ran official red-light districts that for some men became an outlet for feminine company. The Ginza was the Times Square of Tokyo with its vibrant and bustling night life.

After a year on duty, I was eligible for an R & R leave. I enjoyed a long holiday weekend at one of the Army's plush resort venues. It was two hours from the hustle and bustle of Tokyo, close to Mount Fujiyama, and set among five lakes and a mountain. While there, I hiked a trail that ran along the west side of the volcano, and enjoyed the superb accommodations.

I had a spacious studio with large picture windows that afforded me views of nature from every angle.

The food and beverages served at the resort were superb. Selections ranged from traditional western beef and chicken to Japanese noodle and fish dishes. I enjoyed steaks, lobsters, sushi, and a variety of tasty Japanese sakes (rice wines) whose names I have long forgotten. As I think back on that time, I recall that the dining rooms were set with white table linens, napkins, and the finest china and cutlery. We G.I.s and our guests were pampered by Japanese wait staff who were attentive, polite and professional. Jazz trios played nightly in cabarets, and larger ensemble groups provided instrumental and vocal music for our dancing and listening pleasure. It reminded me of a club on 42nd street in New York that I used to visit before joining the Army.

Outdoor recreational opportunities including horseback riding were available to us as well. I remember enjoying the peace and tranquility of the Japanese countryside while riding horseback along trails near the resort, and one afternoon, I invited a young lady to accompany me on a ride. She was a Department of Army Civilian (DAC) and director of the motor pool for the Tokyo-Yokohama area. Maxine was tall, thin and curvy, and dressed like a model out of Vogue magazine. As the guys said at that time, she was a real "dish" (a "10" in today's parlance). I still can recall the strong smell of the Chanel No. 5 she wore that day, and on the other days we met. Most evenings she would send a jeep for me, and we would hang out late into the night. Curfew was at 11:00 p.m., but I never had to be concerned about the guards checking my leave pass when I returned to base. The jeep she arranged would routinely pass through the guard gate at any hour of the night. No questions were asked. Lucky me!

I thought Maxine was always "on point," but her focus was on finding a husband. She wasn't to be in my future because I was 22 and had plans to continue my education: I was not ready for marriage. Two months after I was discharged from the service, by happenstance I picked up a copy of the Baltimore Afro-American newspaper. A headline on the front page of the society section caught my eye: "STOP THE WEDDING!" it read. Below it the was a picture of my old friend Maxine. Her hands were raised in the air, and she appeared very upset. As it turned out, she was at the church to protest the wedding of her fiancé to another woman: He had jilted her some months before. Before the wedding ceremony could proceed, Maxine had to be escorted forcibly from the church. No doubt Maxine had other plans for that guy! As I said, she was a woman who was always "on point!"

NEW YORK UNIVERSITY

After my tour of duty, I returned to the mainland and was discharged from the Army at Fort Meade, Maryland. Fort Meade was where I had been inducted into the service. My mustering out pay was three hundred and fifteen dollars. It was shortly before noon, and a white buddy of mine asked me to have lunch with him. We had on our uniforms, but when we entered a restaurant and sat down to be served, we were refused lunch because I was black. I couldn't understand how this could happen after serving my country and risking my life for all Americans.

I went home and started getting information for graduate schools. I wanted to go to New York because I had a sister living in the Bronx. I thought it would be cheaper to stay with her and her family, so I applied to Columbia University but was not admitted. New York University admitted me on the condition that I made all A's and no B's the first term, a challenge I readily took on. I met it, and showed that I had the academic ability to pursue an advanced degree. I took three courses that spring, one of which was titled, "Selected Topics in Biology." This was a weeding-out course, and it was very rigorous; the other two were less demanding. There must have been fifty former G.I.s in the selected topics course, and not all made the grade. Students had to pass all three courses, and if not, they were out. I passed, and was accepted into further study.

Living in New York was very expensive. I stayed with my sister and her family to save on costs. The G.I. Bill only covered tuition and books, so I had to find a job. I landed one with the New York City Health Department on 14th Street and East River Drive. I worked in the Bacteriology Department, helping to prepare agar media for the bacteriology tests. I worked from 9 a.m. to 4 p.m., Mondays through Fridays. During the week, I had dinner at a Horn and Hardart automat or at Natick's Restaurant on 14th Street before my classes, which started at 6:00 p.m.

Classes were over at 10:00 p.m., so I had to take the number two train to Prospect Avenue in the Bronx where my sister lived. Her husband was a superintendent of an eight-floor building. Their apartment had two bedrooms, a kitchen, a sleep away couch in the living room, and a bathroom. It was an old building that was poorly lit but had heat fueled by coal.

I paid my fair share for room and board and helped my sister in other ways, too. It was quite a challenge financially when combined with expenses related to work and school were included. However, I often said to myself, "No one said it would be easy."

What I paid my sister helped her with taking care of her two daughters. After about five years, they were able to get a "railroad apartment" on the first floor of the building, which gave me an opportunity to have my own room. (Railroad apartments, for those not familiar with the term, are apartments with a series of rooms connecting to each other in a line.) During this time, I kept taking courses at NYU at the downtown, uptown, and New York Aquarium campuses.

I earned my M.S. degree in 1957 and decided to continue studying for a Ph.D. It was very difficult because I had to study on the subway and anywhere I could. In 1958, I took a civil service exam to be a Junior Scientist for New York State, passed it, and subsequently was employed at Downstate Medical Center in Brooklyn, where I met Connie Glasgow, my future wife.

THE STRIKE IN MY HOMETOWN

Using legal challenges in the 1940's, Thurgood Marshall, Oliver W. Hill, William Hastie, Spottswood Robinson III, and Leonard Ransom were gradually winning civil rights cases based upon Federal constitutional challenges. Among the cases was the one in my hometown, *Davis v. County School Board of Prince Edward County (1951)*, which had been initiated by some of the students whom I had taught. They stepped forward to protest the deplorable conditions at the Robert Moton High School in Farmville, Virginia, my hometown.

On April 23, 1951, a two-week, student-led strike spurred an NAACP lawsuit challenging Prince Edward County's racially segregated school system. The students and teachers at Moton were sick, tired, and weary of being expected to learn in an overcrowded, dilapidated, and potbelly stove-heated school building. Led by Barbara Johns, the sixteen-year-old niece of Reverend Vernon Johns—preacher, civil rights advocate, farmer, educator, and father—some 450 students walked out of school and down to School Superintendent T.J. McIllwaine's office to "improve" the conditions at the Moton School. Unfortunately, they were not successful in persuading him and other town officials to acknowledge these inequities and to begin the process of rectifying them. NAACP lawyers Hill and Robinson arrived two days later, however, and convinced the students and community leaders to allow them to file suit for a completely integrated school system rather than just better facilities for Moton. Their lawsuit *Davis v County School Board of Prince Edward County* was filed about one month later, and became part of the historic *Brown v. Board of Education* case that the Warren Court decided on May 17, 1954. The court concluded that "separate educational facilities are inherently unequal," and that racial segregation of schools was a violation of the Equal Protection Clause of the Fourteenth Amendment of the United States Constitution. This ruling paved the way for the integration of public schools nationwide and was a major victory for the civil rights movement. A monument honoring the students involved in the strike is now on the Virginia State Capital grounds near the governor's mansion in Richmond. Among the five cases decided under *Brown v. Board of Education*, *Davis v. County School Board* was the only one initiated by students themselves.

After the decision, there continued to be much resistance to providing integration and equal opportunities in the school system, however. Rather than integrate the schools, Virginia's white segregationists adopted the stance of "Massive Resistance," closing the public schools of many Virginia counties between 1959 and 1964 rather than integrating them. During this period, black students in PEC (some of whom were my relatives) had to go to makeshift schools or forego education altogether. To get around the barriers established by "Massive Resistance," some schools were established in church basements in town, and others were run by groups such as the Society of Friends, outside of the financial support of the state.

Nonetheless, Massive Resistance negatively affected the education of many students of color. Some students had to be bussed out of county to other school districts, and others stopped attending. Some left the state altogether to complete their high school education. In 1964, the final year of

Massive Resistance, the NAACP sponsored Prince Edward Free School to help educate the black youths who had been unable to leave the county or attend public school elsewhere. But, despite the best efforts of countless groups, many students missed part or all of their education for these five years. Civil rights historians have named this era "the lost generation" in Virginia. Although I was and am a son of Prince Edward County, I was helpless to aid in the struggle at that time.

Fifty years after many Virginia public schools shut their doors rather than accept black students, the state started offering college scholarships to compensate those whose education was denied and who suffered during the "massive resistance to desegregation." A person was eligible to apply if he or she had been a domiciled resident of the commonwealth of Virginia or a student not only of PEC but of the majority white schools of Arlington, Charlottesville, Norfolk, and Warren counties at the time of "massive resistance." To my surprise, some of the scholarship recipients were white! The scholarship program represented more than compensation for schooling disruptions—it was also an acknowledgement that segregation was immoral. In my view, offering the scholarship to white students attending schools in the counties noted above diluted the anti-segregationist intent of the *Brown v Board* decision.

While all this was occurring, I was a graduate student at New York University, studying toward a Ph.D. in Biology. Born in Prince Edward County, having attended and taught at Robert R. Moton, I felt helpless to effect change in person. I sympathized with what was going on but having to work full-time and pursue an advanced degree was not easy for me, so I couldn't join the protests.

It took ten years for me to earn a M.S. and Ph.D. in Biology. I still don't know how I did it. It took divine guidance, strength, hope, hard work, and perseverance. I felt that my personal battlefields were on pursuing an advanced degree and surviving in New York City. There was no choice but to let others engage "the enemy" while I did my part on another front. I knew that once I received my degrees, I would be able to make a substantial contribution to the cause of social justice and equal opportunity.

As I am writing, my eyes are filled with tears of thanks and sorrow over the turbulent years in my home town. I get very emotional because having grown up in the church, studying the Bible, and learning the Golden Rule "do unto others as you would have others do unto you," it is hard to comprehend the hate, bigotry, and hurt in many people's hearts at that time.

In May of 1963, I defended my thesis for my Ph.D. in Biology at New York University. I did not participate in the graduation ceremony in June because I was busy at the time. My Ph.D. diploma was mailed to me in October in a long tube that was sent by certified mail. I wasn't concerned about missing the June ceremony because in 1957, I participated in the one for my master's degree.

NEW YORK UNIVERSITY AND FULL-TIME WORK

I lived on Prospect Avenue, a predominantly Afro-American and Latino neighborhood, during my 10 years of graduate study. Each day, I rode the subway to Downstate Medical School in Brooklyn. After my work day I took the subway to NYU in Manhattan. My work day began at nine in the morning and ended at 4:00pm, and my classes began at 6:00pm. The class that started at 6:00 p.m. would be followed by a second class starting at 8:00pm and ending at 10:00pm. Following classes, I had to travel to the Bronx. I used the one-hour ride on the train to study. When I got home, I was exhausted. I found time to complete assignments and study on weekends, during lunch breaks, and whenever I had an opportunity. Social life was virtually non-existent, although occasionally I went to the Savoy Ball room in Harlem where cocktail parties were sponsored by the alumni chapter of Virginia Union University.

My work-study routine defined my life from 1953 to 1963. There were very few graduate fellowships that covered tuition and provided a stipend in those years. The only students that had fellowships were students who were friendly with their professors and served as teaching assistants. There was the G.I. Bill and jobs outside of the university to take care of room, board, transportation, and other needs. I did not have extra money to live on. We only received money for tuition and books. I can recall that transportation was quite difficult because I had a thesis adviser whose office was located at the uptown campus of NYU (Washington Heights) while I attend classes downtown in Greenwich Village.

My advisor was R.P. Hall, a senior faculty member who had written an excellent book in his field, protozoology. We had many lively discussions about my research work. He was very gentle and shy, but also very helpful. He encouraged me to hold on and keep the faith. He believed my day would come. I trusted him and worked very hard to contribute to the scholarly literature in biology. Many of the other graduate students in his class complained that he "mumbled" when he lectured, but it did not bother me. I overlooked his mumbling, and we became good friends. I finally completed all of my Master's thesis requirements for my Master's degree. I then had to take a qualifying exam before I could be considered a candidate for a Ph.D. degree.

The exam was a two-day, four-hour session in the morning and again in the afternoon. I took five to six weeks off from my job (vacation time I had earned), stayed home, and studied everything I could to prepare for it. It was a comprehensive exam covering all of biology, plants, and animals. On the first day of the exam, from eight to noon, I felt that I had answered all the questions satisfactorily. I went to lunch and returned for the afternoon session that lasted until 5:00pm. At the end of this session, I felt I had performed well. The next day, I had a very good feeling in the morning session. After the last session, I was still feeling very good. I thought to myself, "If I don't pass this exam, I am going to shoot someone." Luckily, I did not have to do that. About a month later, I received a notice saying that I had successfully completed the preliminaries. The next step was to continue working on my thesis and to have it reviewed for defense. That took about two more years. My advisor reviewed my thesis and made suggestions about how to strengthen it. I followed his advice. In those days, one had to hire a typist and submit five copies to the department.

The day finally came for my thesis defense. There were six professors and invited guests in my field. All had read my work, and I was questioned about it for about forty minutes, fully prepared to defend any part. I think they voted that day and said, "Congratulations! You did it." I was elated.

What I remember most were those bitter cold winter nights when I had to walk from the subway station to the campus. It was almost ten blocks up a steep hill. Walking in the snow and blustery wind took a toll on me and other students. After taking classes uptown, I still had to go from the west side of Manhattan all the way to the Bronx.

Looking back, I really don't know where the energy, strength, courage, dedication, and focus to reach my goals came from. Maybe it was a built-in habit over the years. In those days, I had no idea where all of this would end and if there would be a personal reward. I refused to think too much about this, however. I kept my own mind clear and "kept my eye on the prize," earning a Ph.D. in Biology. My inner drive to study and work hard could have been divine guidance. I thoroughly enjoyed my graduate courses in biology at NYU, and it was a pleasure to work with such outstanding scholars. I did not make many good friends during my graduate years, because there was no time to socialize. Most of the students had returned from military service, were married, and had families and jobs. While completing my Ph.D., I met a girl that caught my eye: Constance Lenore Glasgow. We met at Downstate Medical Center where she was a medical student working toward completion of her M.D. in the field of pediatrics. Our relationship blossomed, and we decided to marry in 1962.

MEXICO CITY TO SCHENECTADY

Post-Doctoral Studies

In 1962, I applied for a U.S. Public Health Fellowship in Tropical Diseases (Parasitology), and I was one of five Americans accepted. It was a great experience, strengthening my background in my chosen fields, and giving me the opportunity to learn about Latin America.

In late 1962, my wife had completed her medical residency training, and in 1963, we decided to spend a year at the National Medical School in Mexico City. We planned a six-week trip by car before I reported for duty. As we traveled across the country, we visited many National Parks and made good friends along the way. I had a new Toyota (the "automaker of the year"), and we enjoyed it. We stopped at Claremont College in California, where I had an interview for a teaching position. I was soon offered the job but declined it for personal reasons. We wanted to be on the East Coast. We finally arrived in Mexico City around noon and stayed in a hotel for a couple of days until we could find an apartment.

The first night there, however, I had a real introduction to Montezuma's Revenge. I had a light lunch around 2:00pm, but shortly thereafter felt nauseous and started running to the bathroom with diarrhea and vomiting. The owner promised to bring an herbal remedy and hot water bottle to help me.

He said, "Mas tarde. Un momento," but I need his help right away. I was sick all night, but finally my bowels quieted down. The next day, we were offered an apartment with two bedrooms, kitchen and bath on the second floor at Unidad Esperanza, a middle-income Mexican housing unit. We went to bed early that evening around midnight but were awakened by a band of Mariachis serenading us with romantic boleros for 30 minutes. It was a nice way to welcome us. We will never forget it.

Mexico has all kinds of tropical and infectious diseases. In fact, our neighbors across the hall often complained, "Me duele me hídago (my liver hurts)," telling us to be careful about the water and what and where we ate. My wife prepared lunch for me to take to school each day. She would buy apples, place them in a sudsy solution, and give them to me for a snack. As I ate the apples, soap bubbles often came out of my mouth—unforgettable moments!

During our year in Mexico City, the professional background that I had received in Japan was further enriched by the research and clinical work that I conducted in the fellowship program. I had an opportunity to visit and work in endemic areas of malaria, *leishmaniasis*, Chagas disease, and *onchocerciasis*.

When my wife and I had weekends off, we visited some of the amazing archeological sites in Mexico. Teotihuacán was one of our favorite sites where we collected hundreds of reproductions of Pre-Columbian artifacts that we brought to back to America. We now proudly display them in our home.

The research, training, and ability to communicate and learn another culture served me well when I came to Union. I did not come to Union lacking experience in my field or in the ability to convey my ideas to others. I drew upon the broad experience I had gained in the NY City Department of Health at Downstate Medical Center, at the 406th Medical Laboratory in

Tokyo, and during my fellowships in Mexico and Central America to develop my course lectures and laboratory exercises. Many of my colleagues today had and still have no idea of what I brought to the biology department at Union. I was not an inexperienced assistant professor, and had no time to prove myself to anybody, so I did my work and invested my time forging positive relationships with students.

During the summer of my second year at Union, I was awarded the Tropical Medicine Fellowship sponsored by the State of Louisiana in all medical and biological disciplines relating to parasitology and tropical medicine. The American subtropics presented unique opportunities to study the clinical, laboratory, and epidemiological problems of most infectious diseases. The program covered basic parasitology, virology, bacteriology, protozoology, mycology, public health, biostatistics, epidemiology, medical entomology, and nutrition. It aimed to acquaint us with the status of research relevant to the existing health problems in the region. I was one of five selected for this exclusive program to meet with the Louisiana State staff of the U.S. Public Service Hospital for Hansen's Disease in Carville, Louisiana. The program lasted for eight weeks.

As part of the program, I visited countries in Central America including Honduras, El Salvador, Guatemala, and Costa Rica. Malaria, transmitted by the bite from an infected mosquito, was a recurring plague in Mexico. Malaria presents itself with flu-like symptoms including fevers, chills, headache, and general fatigue. If left untreated, it can cause death.

One interesting organism that my students had not heard of before was the "kissing bug." *American trypanosomiasis* (Chagas disease) is the most common lethal infectious parasitic disease in the Western Hemisphere. Chagas heart disease is considered incurable and is a leading cause of death in rural areas of Latin America. Moreover, numerous studies have documented the presence of many intestinal organisms in young adults in parts of Central America. These parasitic worm infections are associated with malnutrition and malaria.

In endemic areas in Mexico, people lived in thatch-roofed homes. During the day, an insect called the reduviid bug or "kissing bug" found refuge in the thatched roofs and walls of homes. At night, it emerged to quietly bite sleeping humans, giving rise to high fever, swollen glands, and other symptoms that would disappear after several weeks. At this stage,the number of trypanosomes in the blood would decrease, but over time the parasite would persist, multiply, and wiggle out to invade and destroy neighboring cells. Eventually, the infection would severely damage the heart and gastrointestinal tract or cause debilitating gastrointestinal disease. Death from Chagas disease sometimes takes a decade after infection and can be swift and ugly. Infection may produce irregular heartbeat, congestive heart failure, and stroke.

My time spent in Japan and with individuals in Mexico was a building block for my professionalism, as well as an opportunity for me to learn about different cultures. When I arrived at Union, I was well-prepared for my teaching responsibilities, but no one had any idea of my research background nor did they care. My colleagues were busy making sure that their courses were full and that they were taking care of the politics within the department and the college. I was not interested in college politics nor did I have the time to waste.

I was awarded tenure because I worked very hard. I focused my energy on preparing my lectures and laboratory exercises. I feel that a good teacher brings out the natural talent of a student. I also believe that people have different ways of mastering material. I exposed my students to lecture and discussion sessions, strong laboratory work, excellent textbooks and other reading materials, preserved and live specimens, and life-like models and visual aids to help them learn parasitology.

I maintained my students' attention by telling them real-life stories of people I had encountered while travelling or at home. During my service with the 406th, doctors thought that a man who loved sashimi (raw fish) had appendicitis until a surgeon cut him open, found his appendix was fine, and spotted a worm crawling from his abdomen as they were about to sew him up (it turned out to be a parasitic roundworm). The lesson is that people should be wary of eating sashimi and some varieties of sushi now served in many restaurants and supermarkets across America. These and other worms may cause serious complications if they perforate the intestine or stomach. When consumers eat these Japanese delicacies, or ceviche, gravlax, or inadequately cooked meats or unwashed vegetables they potentially expose themselves to several types of worm infections. I always tried to raise my students' awareness of the risks associated with food-borne diseases. They are not on most people's radar when they are enjoying good food with good company. Fortunately, I have dealt with parasites for seventy years but luckily have never been infected by one...at least to my knowledge!

In addition, my laboratory exercises were designed to coordinate and enhance the material presented in lectures. I wanted them to be as realistic and as hands-on as possible, so I had my students work with malaria in mice, trypanosomes in rats, roundworms in mice, and tapeworms in rats. We would inject the rats with cysticercoids (larval stages of tapeworms) found in the flower beetle. The cysticercoids would then be placed on slides and examined under a microscope. Students were intrigued to see that these organisms looked like tennis rackets! By the end of the term, students would be able to recover from the rats the cysticercoids that had developed into two- to three-foot long adult tapeworms. Their eyes would then light up and became as large as saucers after witnessing how much the tapeworms had grown. I tried to teach them about parasites using experiments that they would never forget.

I also taught them how to anesthetize and inoculate mice humanely and safely. I wanted them to learn and understand these techniques so that they would be well-prepared for medical and graduate school. I never had a problem with attendance in my courses because my enthusiasm and love of the subject matter was obvious to them. I tried to "fire them up" and keep them focused. One day, a young man came to class with an eight-inch roundworm in a large jar and gave it to me. It was an *Ascaris lumbricoides* (the most common parasitic roundworm found in humans). He had contracted it while on a term abroad. I preserved the worm in 10% formalin and placed his name on it. It was added to my extensive collection of organisms. On another occasion, a young lady taking the course told me she had been having diarrhea for a week, and it wouldn't stop. I asked her to bring in a stool specimen. She had learned the laboratory procedure for preparing stool specimens so she performed it and looked under the microscope to diagnose herself: she had contracted *Giardia Lamblia,* a protozoan usually found in food or water contaminated by mammalian feces. I confirmed her self-diagnosis, and recommended that she see a doctor. She was treated and soon returned to class, smiling from ear-to-ear and knowing that what she learned in biology class had real-world applications.

On another occasion, a male student came to me with something very tiny in a jar. We put it under a magnifying glass and saw something that resembled a crab. He found it in the genital region of his pubic hair, and it looked like a six-legged snail. The front two legs resembled the pincher claws of a crab, and lo and behold he had contracted crab lice, a sexually transmitted disease. He apparently had had intimate relations with a coed from a local college, so he sought medical help, and then was successfully treated by his doctor. I never told the rest of the class about his story because I considered the teacher-student relationship to be as confidential as a doctor-patient one. If my students volunteered to share their encounters and personal experiences with the class for educational purposes, they were welcomed to do so, but I never pushed them to.

I also supervised many students who did independent research projects that resulted in a thesis proper. Their final projects were reviewed by two other professors in the department as well, and required the approval of all three of us to earn passing grades. Some independent research projects were nominated for honors at graduation.

 I focused on my students' growth and development, and always had an open-door policy. Students could meet me after class, in hallways, or in dining areas to discuss their concerns. My goal was to provide them with a foundational education that they could use in graduate school. Nurturing my students' academic and personal growth during their time at Union was immensely rewarding and satisfying to me.

I had some of the finest students one could have in a course. Those who did independent research with me were the best. They chose to work with me after taking one of my courses, and they applied what they learned in my courses to their own projects. Typically, it took a year and a summer to complete a project. I remember supervising a student who performed independent research with me (and later, his sister, as well). My wife and I were pleasantly surprised to be invited to his doctoral graduation and then to his wedding. The wedding was just like Hollywood, and it was held in Buckhead, Atlanta, Georgia. When we arrived, we were greeted in our hotel room by a gift basket with champagne and candies. That evening, the groom hosted a dinner reception at an exclusive country club with membership limited to only the rich. When we went to the reception in this huge ballroom, there were two movie screens: One was showing *The Way We Were* and the other, *Gone with the Wind*. The groom handed out NY Giants baseball caps and the bride passed out Atlanta Braves caps. It was an evening of fun and games. The next day, we had lunch at a writer's home in Buckhead and toured his estate, resplendent with flowers, manicured lawns, and all the accoutrements that go with wealth.

A JOB OFFER IN SCHENECTADY

In the late 40s, there were no NIH (National Institute for Health), NSF (National Science Foundation) scholarships, or other resources to help blacks pay for a college education. We black students had to work to pay for our education. Back then, most blacks were not able to get a loan because we had no collateral. Despite these financial obstacles, we were able to succeed because our driving force was the hope that someday things would get better and that we could have a better quality of life than our forebears. When I graduated from college and graduate school, I did not owe anyone a dime: I was free to pursue employment I desired.

The first time I heard of General Electric was when I was teaching high school. After my first year (1948-9), I received a Westinghouse Science Teachers Fellowship to spend six weeks at MIT enrolled in a science course designed for high school teachers. One day, Union College came up in a conversation that I had with a friend who had received a six-week General Electric-sponsored fellowship to study humanities at Union. He told me a little about Schenectady and about Union College. He said that he liked Union but that there wasn't much for blacks to do in Schenectady.

I was planning on travelling by bus to MIT since I did not own a car at the time. I took the bus from Farmville to Washington, D.C., where I met a teacher who was driving to Cambridge, MA. On the way, we stopped in New York City and saw Rodgers and Hammerstein's Broadway hit *South Pacific*. It starred Ezio Pinza, Mary Martin, and Juanita Hall. It was such a superb production that I will never forget it. When the character Bloody Mary sang, "Bali Hai," never did I dream that one day I would have the opportunity to travel to the island of Bali, which I did in my 60s. It seems that many of the experiences that I encountered along life's way were preordained.

Fast forward 17 years to Mexico. When we left Mexico City early on the morning of August 23rd, 1965, we were headed for Brooklyn. The day we left, Mexico City experienced one of its worse earthquakes ever, a magnitude 8.1 on the Richter scale. We had lived in Mexico City for one year while I completed my post-doctoral Fellowship in the Department of Human Ecology at the National Medical School. I learned about the job at Union when I returned from a field trip to Chiapas, Mexico, about a week before we left. We had spent the day studying "river blindness" (*onchocerciasis*), a disease found in the tropics transmitted by human-biting black flies. In many individuals, the infection produces little or no disease, but those with heavy infections usually exhibited three cardinal manifestations: eye lesions, dermatitis, and subcutaneous nodules. More than 17.7 million people worldwide are infected, and visual impairment occurs in 500,000 of them.

I was part of a team of medical doctors, nurses, entomologists, ecologists, parasitologists and natives who carried in our equipment and medical supplies to treat patients who lived in a rural area of Chiapas. The parasite-endemic area was located on the side of a very steep mountainside. We were scheduled to leave at 8:00 a.m., but the group departed much later in the morning down a steep mountainside with tropical foliage and small streams rushing by. We had donned our boots and carried our water bottles, and everyone had something to take: food, water, medicine, or first aid supplies. As we descended this rugged path to the designated area, we were surprised at how long it was taking us to arrive at the village where the family we were going to study lived. It took us two hours instead of the 30 minutes we had planned for! When we arrived around noon, we unpacked our gear and had lunch. Around 2:00 p.m., we started observing the father, mother, and children. The doctor said that their conditions occurred from inflammatory responses in the anterior portion of the eye as a result of the degenerative effects of microfilaria (parasites) in their eyes.

We then examined the subcutaneous nodules on their bodies and took samples of tissue for processing. At around 4:00 p.m., the sky was covered with darkness, and we knew that a tropical storm was imminent. It took us a while to gather our equipment for our trek back up the mountain. As we started our return up the mountain, the sky opened into a tropical downpour and in less than three minutes, everyone was soaked and water was gushing down our path like a river. It had taken us two hours to walk down to the valley where the family resided, and with darkness descending, I wondered if we would ever get back to the top of the mountain where we had parked our van. Moreover, the light from our flashlights attracted swarms of bats that menaced us as we climbed. There were four groups of scientists, each led by a local guide. I was in the second group, and at about 8:00 p.m., we stopped to wait for the third group because only they knew how to get to the top. My group finally arrived at the top at 10:00 p.m., but group three arrived about one hour later because one of their scientists was suffering from cardiac problems, and our guide had to go back to help them carry him up the mountain. A little after midnight, the last—and, as it turned out, most important—group arrived: the doctor and nurse in this last group were the only ones that had a key to the van! Also, as it turned out, I "saved" the night: knowing we were going to a dangerous area, I had brought a fifth of scotch for "medicinal purposes." The tired, hungry, and weary scientists thanked me for sharing it with everyone: we downed it in a matter of minutes. (Footnote: Later, I was told that the married doctor and his nurse part-ner were responsible for our leaving late the morning of the trip and con-sequently getting stuck in the downpour!)

Later during our stay in Mexico, Dr. Edward Berg, a parasitologist from the State University at New York (SUNY) at Albany, informed me about an opening at Union College and urged me to apply for the position. Mem-ories of talking with my friend who was awarded a General Electric hu-manities fellowship came flooding back to mind. I began to gather information and think seriously about Union. I discovered that it had been founded in 1795 and was the second oldest private institution chartered in New York State. I decided to apply for the job at Union, and shortly there-after received a letter asking me to come for an interview.

When Connie and I arrived in Schenectady for the job interview, the first building on campus we saw was the Nott Memorial. The Nott Memorial Center is the architectural and physical centerpiece of the campus. I looked at it from the outside and thought, "This is the place where I would like to be." I had never before seen a sixteen-sided, stone-carved building. It was a stately and majestic edifice. The 110-foot (34 m) high by 89-foot (27 m) wide structure was and still is a National Historic Landmark. Moreover, the campus appeared to be one conducive to learning, creativity, and growth. Nott Memorial was restored during the Union College presidency of Roger Hull (1990-2005), and during his tenure, it was rumored that it was going to be torn down. President Hull's vision was to have the Nott Memorial re-stored to its original grandeur: He did the architectural research and raised the money to accomplish his vision. It's truly a remarkable building.

On another note, I will never forget that on my way to the interview in 1965, I received my first speeding ticket between exits 18 and 19 on the New York State Thruway: I was in a rush to make it on time. Once I arrived on campus, I met with Dr. Leonard Clark, Chairman of the Department of

Biological Sciences. I spent two hours with him and was offered the position on the same day! I only had about ten days to move to Schenectady before the fall semester began. After the interview, a young professor greeted me and spent about five minutes with us. He handed me the classified ads of the *Schenectady Gazette* (the local newspaper), and admonished me to "stay off the hill." At the time, I didn't understand what "the hill" was, but later I found out that it was Hamilton Hill, a notoriously underprivileged area of Schenectady riddled by drugs and violence. I heeded his warning.

GUESS WHO'S MOVING TO SCHENECTADY?

Connie and I began to pour over local newspapers for a place to live as soon as possible. Many of the leading realtors would not show us homes in certain zip codes because these areas were occupied primarily by whites. Restrictive (racist) covenants were in full force in those days, and even though there were three apartment houses on Union Avenue just across from the college that had large "For Rent" signs on the lawn, none of them rented to us. When our white friend, Professor Malcolm Willison of the Sociology Department checked the actual availability of the apartments, they were not actually rented. Restrictive covenants typically stipulated the following: "hereafter no part of said property or any portion thereof shall be occupied by a person not of the Caucasian race, it being intended hereby to restrict the use of the said property for residence or other purposes by people of the Negro or Mongolian race." Our difficulty in finding housing was a forecast of things to come in Schenectady. Needless to say, it was very difficult to prepare for classes while not having a place to live.

Fortunately, for a short period of time, we were "saved" by a couple who had a summer cottage in the Plattekill area of Rotterdam. It was a four-room structure that had a bedroom, living room, kitchen, and shower. There was a cistern to gather rainwater for showers. For three weeks after classes had begun, however, we had to carry gallons of bottled water from the Union College biology department for us to drink and cook with.

Needless to say, it was hard to concentrate on my teaching duties while living under these conditions. During the third week of September, the temperature dropped into the forties at night, and we were cold because the cottage was not insulated. The next day, I told Dr. Clark that we were going to leave Union because of the living conditions. We told him that it was inhumane for anyone to be treated this way, and thank goodness he was able to come through for us. The next day, he told us about an apartment on Wendell Avenue offered for rent by a Union College graduate and prominent lawyer in Schenectady. The apartment was in his home, and we eagerly took it.

UNION COLLEGE

When I arrived at Union, the college was on a two-semester calendar. The department offered two-semester courses each year in Comparative Anatomy, Embryology, Physiology, Genetics, Botany, Invertebrate Anatomy, and Human Biology for non-majors. All had a laboratory component. During my first semester at Union, I taught introductory biology, parasitology, and a laboratory in comparative anatomy. In 1980, I organized and taught the first immunology course with laboratory, and offered several elective courses, two of which were titled, "Nutrition, Health and Diseases," and "*In Vitro* Fertilization for non-majors."

Before I arrived at Union, the Trustees decided to increase the size of the student body. A new Dean of Science & Engineering was appointed, a new science and engineering center was planned, and a focus on faculty and student research was emphasized. The College also increased faculty recruitment and research funds and reduced teaching loads to lighten the burden on new faculty in particular. Early in my career, I was appointed to the committee responsible for designing a curriculum suited for a trimester calendar. We also worked to establish a new set of required courses for all undergraduates.

In 1970, we moved into our Science and Engineering Center as proud as peacocks. The new laboratory facilities, research facilities, and equipment had put us in the pedagogical vanguard for small liberal arts colleges. I knew this was the case because in 1973 I served as an evaluator of small liberal arts colleges for the Middle States Evaluation Team. I realized how fortunate Union was in having the support of the administration in making it a premier institution at which to study the sciences. Our department was a leader in the breath of biology courses it offered, as well as in the depth of its teaching and research.

I came to the biology department in 1965 and between 1967 and 1971, the department grew rapidly with the addition of six new tenure-track faculty positions. In addition, more independent research opportunities for students were added to the biology curriculum. Moreover, we started an honors program to afford students the opportunity to work one-on-one with a faculty advisor for a year on a research project culminating in an undergraduate thesis. To receive credit, students had to earn the approval of their advisor and of two other faculty members. Students who did exceptional work were nominated for departmental honors and recognized at the graduation ceremony at the end of the year.

Faculty and students formed close relationships in our department, and I enjoyed motivating students to do undergraduate research and independent study. Many of the students who have done independent research with me are now doctors, university professors, and research scientists. It is always a joy to hear from them and to know that what they learned in my classes had a profound impact on their choice of careers. They tell me that they appreciate having learned the laboratory techniques used in our classes: immunofluorescence, immunochemistry, monoclonal antibodies, and how to humanely care for and use animals in research.

Moreover, I tried to make our laboratories informative and practical. I always kept abreast of the literature and incorporated the latest technologies that we had the funds and space to procure. I also tried my best to position my students to be in the vanguard of their disciplines: I required them to write laboratory reports, present research papers, and critique the research of their classmates. I feel happy that many of them told me then and even today that they were able to get summer employment because of what they learned in our laboratories.

Before I go any further, I must say that much of my good start at Union College should be attributed to Dr. Leonard Clark, the man who hired me and served as my first department chair. A tall, slender native of Canada, Dr. Clark was very kind and gracious to Connie and me. He invited us to his home for dinner, introduced us to some prominent members of the community, and supported us 100 percent. Unfortunately, in 1967, he and his wife retired and moved to Cape Cod. I'll never forget how much he helped me, and will always remember him favorably.

EARLY LIFE IN CLIFTON PARK

Connie became pregnant in 1966, and we knew that we would have to find living quarters larger than those offered to us in Schenectady. A colleague of mine in the biology department then invited us to visit his best friend in Clifton Park, and we told him that we were having problems finding adequate housing. He suggested that we talk with Mr. Robert Van Patten, a prominent housing developer in Clifton Park. We wanted a house large enough so that we could have a home as well as a pediatric office that Connie could open a solo practice from. We met Robert Van Patten, told him what we wanted, and he replied, "I will build anything you want. We would be glad to have you out here in Clifton Park!" Those were the sweetest words I had heard in a long time. We met with him in the spring of 1967 with our requirements, and decided to choose his largest colonial model with added space for an office. It was a ¾ acre corner lot, so it would be easy for patients to see Connie once she opened her office. Scott was due in July, and I had been awarded a Louisiana State Medical School Tropical Diseases Fellowship to study in Honduras, El Salvador, Costa Rica, Guatemala, and Mexico. Having our housing dilemma solved before leaving on the fellowship was a great weight lifted from our shoulders.

During my fellowship, I studied infectious hepatitis and all kinds of tropical diseases. I accepted this opportunity hoping I would be home when Scott was born, but as it turned out, I was not able to see him for about two weeks. He was born on July 12th, and I was notified a few days later while on a field trip to the rain forest in Costa Rica. In celebration of his arrival, my colleagues treated me to a big Costa Rican dinner with plenty of tequila, and a good time was had by all. I was home towards the end of July, and we moved into our newly built home in Clifton Park in the first week of September of 1967. Connie's mother then came from Brooklyn and stayed with us to help her care for Scott: She was extremely helpful to us at the time and for the remaining years of her life.

In early September, the public schools opened at Shenendehowa, and while I was mowing our lawn one afternoon, a school bus passed loaded with students. Suddenly, a student shouted the "n-word" at me, and it reverberated in my ears loud and clear. I told the friend of ours who had invited us to live in Clifton Park, and he told the superintendent of the Shenendehowa School District. We never heard such language again.

Union College didn't open until two weeks later. To our surprise, only a week after school had just opened at Shenendehowa, its teachers went on strike. The superintendent of schools and the Town Supervisor of Clifton Park then decided to put out the call for volunteer teachers to help keep the schools open. Because I had taught high school biology at Moton High School, I volunteered to teach biology at Shenendehowa High School. As it turned out, many of the people whom Connie and I had first met in Clifton Park were teachers at Shenendehowa. Whether or not this played a role in what happened next, I'll never know.

Nevertheless, on my second day of teaching biology, I was standing in front of the class talking to the students about basic lab techniques when suddenly I smelled a pungent odor. I thought that a mouse had died or something, so I started searching from whence it came. BINGO. I opened the top drawer of my desk and found a big pile of human feces. I reported it to the administrators. Luckily, I did not have but one more day to substitute, so I wasn't too distressed about it, but I distinctly remember having received deep criticism from many of my new "friends" and teachers because I had crossed their picket line to teach their students. Their criticism didn't hurt me, however, because they themselves had never been denied an opportunity to obtain an education. They did not have to attend separate but unequal schools in the South. I am a son of Prince Edward County, Virginia, and I did.

Another unfortunate experience of living in Clifton Park in the early 1970s comes to mind. Auria, our daughter, was born nineteen months after Scott in 1969 and was a bright, happy, energetic, and outgoing child. She enjoyed pre-school and eagerly attended nursery school at the Shenendehowa United Methodist Church (our church home), but three weeks after she entered the first grade, she came home with a headache and looked depressed. I decided to go to her first-grade class and observe what was going on. I discovered after three days that her teacher, a black lady, was as strict as my marine sergeant in the Army. Her students had to march in step and had very little freedom to relax. I had the answer to our problem: Auria simply could not adjust to a classroom that was overly regimented. That Friday, I made an appointment with her school principal at 4:30 p.m. to discuss the matter.

He said, "Sorry, Mr. Styles, we don't have any place to move your daughter."

I looked him in straight in the eye and said, "Sir, get on the phone and call your wife because we are not leaving the building until she is moved." It took him ten minutes to place her in a classroom where learning was less regimented and more interactive. We went home after that.

Scott had some negative experiences, too. One was an encounter in the fifth grade when a boy called him a "nappy headed n—-er." I went to school the next day and talked with his teacher. I told her that we did not teach our children to hate others, so we did not expect hateful comments from others in return. We taught them to respect all people irrespective of their race, creed, ethnicity, or cultural background. She listened to me intently, and I said to her, if this occurs again, "I have authorized him to knock the kid's teeth out, and I will pay for them." It did not happen again.

Having grown up in Farmville, Virginia, I was not surprised at racism being directed at my children. It was only a matter of time. As a child, I was the butt of racist remarks and put downs, and was not going to have my children suffer them without consequence to the perpetrators. As an adult, I, too, experienced racist remarks and innuendos on the street and in stores, was pulled over by the police (a.k.a "driving while black"), and sometimes received ignorant remarks from colleagues. When one experiences such treatment during childhood, in the Army, and throughout one's life, one become keenly sensitive to any slight (i.e., any microaggression). Sometimes I respond, and sometime I don't. I'm always aware of them, however.

My memories of the early years in Clifton Park through the present have reminded me that there have been no new words invented or situations involving race that I have not already experienced. When younger people ask me what to do about them, I tell them to do their best to move on, look forward, and not be discouraged by them. I tell them to do their best to use their energy to achieve the goals they have set for themselves rather than have it depleted by feeling discouraged and angry at ignorant people.

THE HELP

When our children were young, finding qualified individuals to care for them was difficult while we both worked. We went through new nannies about every six months. In those days, it was very difficult to hire locals, so we had to seek people from outside of the United States. Since Connie's parents came from Trinidad and St. Vincent, we looked favorably upon applicants from the Caribbean. We hired several young nannies from Caribbean countries, but once they had a chance to visit friends and relatives in NYC, it was goodbye. One could understand why: There were not many young people of color in our area for them to socialize with.

When the kids were around 7- or 8-years-old, we were fortunate to find a young lady from Austria. Her husband was a student at Union College, and she was looking for something to do. We invited her to help us with our kids and Connie's father, and she did a wonderful job. Crystal became a member of our family, and we opened our home to her and her husband. One amongst many gifts she gave to our family was teaching our kids how to ski. Being from Austria, she was an expert skier (she fulfilled the stereotype!), and taught both Scott and Auria how to ski. Today, both of them are competent skiers (Auria more so than Scott, by his own admission), and they owe their first coach, Crystal, a debt of gratitude for her instruction. She returned to Austria some thirty years ago but has still kept in touch with us.

TEACHING, LEARNING AND MENTORING

Teaching has changed since I came to Union in 1965. The curriculum now includes more liberal learning seminars, an emphasis on student-driven research, and the utilization of new technologies that are constantly changing. Nonetheless, I learned while teaching at Union that there is no single method that works to educate all students all the time. The abilities, backgrounds, and needs of students differ widely, and an effective professor must be creative and flexible in his or her approach to teaching.

Undergraduate teaching is a lot of work. I always say, "You earn your paycheck at Union." Laboratory courses are extremely expensive, and independent work requires enormous investments in human and financial resources. My research often required me to work on Saturdays, Sundays, and holidays year-round.

Since the 70s, Union has made a genuine effort to support faculty-mentored student research. One weekend in May is set aside to highlight and showcase this work. At this event, called the Steinmetz Symposium, students across all disciplines show and tell the Union community about their independent research projects. The joy of supervising a student-driven independent biology project is when one sees young mentees opens their "mind vault" and allow their innate abilities to take over. When students gain confidence in themselves to explore their interests, I feel satisfied that I have done my job. It's been said by wise people that the most successful teachers train students who eventually exceed the abilities of their teachers. Whether I have done this or not is not for me to say, but I know I did my best to motivate, encourage, and open pathways of explorations for them.

I had the opportunity to meet many freshmen each academic year, and one young man stands out in my memory. He was from Albany, and in typical freshman fashion, "bright-eyed and bushy tailed," full of life, energy, and expectations. I saw him three weeks later in the hall, but his demeanor had changed. He looked like another person. I asked, "What is wrong? You don't look like yourself. Is there anything I can do to help you?"

He said, "Professor Styles, I just came back from a funeral in South Carolina." I asked him who had passed away. He stated that his father just passed away. His father was shot in Albany, and he had to go down to South Carolina to attend his funeral. What a bombshell! What a way to start off a freshman year in college! I believe he was able to continue his studies at Union and graduate, but I haven't heard from him since then.

This is an example of some of the issues that you must deal with as a professor. In my parasitology classes, I wanted to make students feel free to talk with me privately about their own issues or in class about anything related to the course I was teaching. We had open discussions, we were mature adults, and that's just how it was.

For example, in my parasitology course, we talked about roundworm infection of dogs, and how these parasites could be harmful to humans. If the mother dog had parasites, she could transmit them to her puppies, so it was important that all puppies take medicine to be de-wormed. Unbeknownst to most people, many dogs defecate in parks, on college campuses, or on one's own lawn. When they do, they have the potential to deposit roundworm eggs into the soil. Some young children who put things in their mouths may then ingest these eggs, which may then hatch in the child (although humans are abnormal hosts for roundworms). If viable, the larval stage of these roundworms can then migrate to all parts of the body, particularly the eyes.

A real-life example I told my students about was about a Union College history professor and his wife who bred and raised sheepdogs. When their son was sixteen or seventeen, he started having problems with his eyesight. They took him to the doctor and discovered that he had contracted larval roundworms in his eyes. The young man ended up blind in one eye. Notwithstanding his challenges, he was very smart and was admitted to Harvard.

Examples such as this made my parasitology course interesting and joyful for the students. I showed them living examples of parasites from many hosts so that that they could see and correlate to real-life what we were discussing in theory. They learned from textbooks, lectures, and laboratories. For example, we studied the trypanosomes that cause sleeping sickness in Africa. A nonpathogenic form unique to rats would show students fluctuations in the number of antibodies to the trypanosomes that the rats produced in their blood throughout the course of infection. The students got practice taking blood samples and looking under the microscope to follow the progression of the infection.

They were in awe over what they had achieved and were never bored. If students read information in textbooks or saw color pictures of parasites, it was not the same as if they had looked at it themselves under a microscope or made slides on their own. At the end of each term, students were able to take their slides and preserved specimens home with them to show their friends and parents.

I also served as a master's thesis advisor for many students. This commitment was very time consuming. I met with my advisees on a regular schedule as well as when they needed help solving problems that came up during their studies. My door was always open, and I was never too busy to take time out to talk with a student, whether they were undergraduates or master's students.

THE SHADOW OF DEATH

Life requires that we maintain a balance between family and career. I sadly recall the day my sister's husband passed away in 1986. I arranged to attend his funeral, which was held the following weekend in Amelia, Virginia. I spent much time consoling and supporting her and her two daughters, and had the opportunity to catch up with other relatives attending his funeral. Although it is almost universal that families, during times of grief, share food to console each other, we should all nonetheless watch our diets. I remember indulging heartily in "soul food"—ham, fried chicken, bacon, collard greens, macaroni, corn, fried fish, and peach cobbler: food that in retrospect I should have avoided.

I returned to Clifton Park the following day on Sunday with a full feeling in my chest. I thought it was indigestion that came from my weekend diet. The next day, I told my wife that I was not feeling well. She told me to call our doctor, Dr. Arnold Ritterband, an internist in Schenectady, who had me schedule an appointment for a thorough physical exam as soon as possible. A few days later, I saw him, and he ordered an EKG and stress test. The tests were not definitive enough to make a diagnosis, so he then ordered a thallium stress test and saw some changes in my PT waves which required follow-up with an angiogram.

It was late August, and I thought I would be ready to return to classes in September, but it was not to be. During the angiogram, I could see my heart on the monitor while music by Haydn played in the background. Little did I know at the time that the test was showing that I had four clogged cardiac veins in my left ventricle. Wow! What a scare! The doctor said that I needed coronary bypass surgery as soon as possible and suggested Albany, Cleveland, New York, or Boston. I lived in New York City before coming to Schenectady and had seen the type of care that was given by the support staff at some hospitals there so I ruled it out. Albany Medical Center had not done that many bypasses at the time, and Cleveland was too far from home. So, that left Boston and Brigham and Women's hospital as the only viable choice. It had an excellent success rate, was a national center of coronary care, and performed large numbers of procedures. Coronary bypass surgery is a procedure that restores blood flow to your heart muscle. The bypass surgery uses a healthy blood vessel from the leg, arm, chest, or abdomen and connects it to the other arteries in your heart so that blood is bypassed around the diseased or blocked area. In my case, I didn't experience the traditional symptoms such as chest pain and shortness of breath. The only symptom I had was a feeling of fullness in my chest. Dr. Ritterband saved my life. Had he been less thorough, I would probably not be alive today. *I WAS A WALKING TICKING TIME BOMB FOR A HEART ATTACK.*

The Brigham had some of the best cardiologists in the world and the latest technologies to help cardiac patients survive and live normal lives again. I was given an appointment for October 24th, 1986, the same day I had entered the Army in 1950. I notified the chair of the biology department, and was granted a medical leave to take care of my heart. I arrived one day ahead of the surgery, and the staff did all the necessary preliminary tests. The evening before the surgery, I met with the surgeon and his team.

They assured me that I would be in good professional hands and answered my questions. Dr. John Carter, a world-famous surgeon, performed the surgery. He advised me that the vessel grafts usually last around 13 years. For me, 13 years has turned into 32 years!

My surgery was scheduled for 7:00 a.m., and my wife was there with me. Scott and Auria flew up from Princeton to be with me, too, even though it was during their mid-term exams. I was given an injection to relax. The last thing I remember was feeling groggy and being wheeled on a stretcher down the corridor to the operating room.

When I awoke in the recovery room, Scott was trying to pry my eyes open with his fingers and talk with me. He said, "Dad? Dad?" I could not speak because they had put a tube in my throat to help me breathe, and I was restrained. I stayed in the recovery room for four hours and then I was wheeled to my hospital room. I was monitored around the clock with tubes and IVs everywhere. The second day after surgery, the nurses helped me out of bed to take a few steps. Each day, I felt better and stronger, and on the sixth day, they discharged me. Six weeks later, I attended a Christmas Eve service at our church where I personally gave thanks to God for surviving the surgery. (One thing I distinctly remember from the church service was that the odor from the candles really bothered me, however, and I was glad to return home as soon as it was over.)

During my long recovery, our housekeeper, Pattie, kept an eye on me during the daytime while I was convalescing. We formed a great bond. One day, we were talking about the golden years, and she looked me straight in the eyes and said, "Mr. Styles, the only thing that's golden when you get old is your urine."

My son, Scott, took the winter term off from his studies at Princeton to help with my recovery. He was fortunate to have also been able to take some courses at Union while keeping an eye on me, too. Later in the spring,

Scott came to me and said, "Dad, I've got something to tell you." As a parent, when you hear that from your child, you tremble in your boots.

I asked him, "What is it?"

He replied, "Auria and I are going to send you and Mom on a cruise."

"How much does it cost?" I said. He said, "Nothing. We have pooled our savings and taken care of it. You both deserve it after all you've been through." They had arranged for us to visit Cozumel, Mexico, where there are pre-Columbian ruins, the Grand Cayman Islands, Jamaica, and Labadee, a resort area in Haiti. "We have already worked out the details for you to fly from here and sail from Miami," he said. Needless to say, I was very grateful to them. About a month later, we packed our bags, and went on our first cruise.

Our first port-of-call was Mexico, where we visited the ruins in Cozumel. We had previously visited Teotihuacán, Toluca, and other pre-Columbian archeological sites when we were in Mexico in 1964. From there, we went to the Grand Cayman Islands and marveled at the beaches and the black onyx. Next, we disembarked in Ocho Rios, where we visited waterfalls, and I had the opportunity to play golf. Our last stop was in Labadee, Haiti, an island that was owned by the cruise ship company and a great place to simply relax and enjoy the sun and sand. Overall, the cruise was a wonderful way for me and Connie to get away from it all and restore our spirits after what had been a very challenging year for me and our family.

NURTURING CULTURAL DIVERSITY

The campus of Union College is quiet and beautiful, evoking a place and time of harmony where there were few differences and all strived to live up to the ideals enshrined in Union's founding motto, "Under the laws of Minerva, we all become brothers and sisters." I have been part of the fabric and culture of this small liberal arts college for more than 50 years. In a series of conversations in 1996 with Carl George, my closest friend and fellow long-serving faculty member at Union, it became clear to us that more could be done to make the college a place of true union—a place that minimized barriers of race, class, gender, creed, and sexuality. As a result, Carl and I decided to inaugurate a fund that would encourage and support a campus culture that fully embraced diversity and opportunity. When we retired, we joined forces to establish on June 1, 1997, a campus wide organization whose primary mission is to support and encourage diversity, acceptance, and the celebration of cultural differences. We named it Unitas.

Providing equal opportunities for all students was a challenge not unique to Union, however: The same issues were being dealt with at other colleges and universities. At Union and other places of higher learning, students of color were often regarded as "less than" white students. Minority students often felt that their color, race, or religion were barriers to their achieving their academic goals, despite campus efforts to promote diversity. Students of color, as well as other minority students, often found themselves to be the only ones of their heritage in the classes they took. They frequently felt singled out to represent the minority perspective, and felt very stressed about this "responsibility."

I recall an incident involving the black student takeover of the Union College computer center in the late 1960s. Students occupied the center for several days to highlight their concerns about racist behavior on campus: One incident they condemned was when a white student dressed up in blackface for a Halloween celebration on campus: He had colored his face and hands black and donned a purple jacket and an afro wig. He told students he was dressed as a pimp. Many white students did not understand why putting on a blackface offended the black students on campus. It turned out to be a teachable moment for the campus community, and within a week, more than 100 students and faculty gathered in support of diversity and understanding.

More than 30 years later, Unitas sponsored a Balinese dance group for four days. They performed culturally enriching dances and played the gamelan and other traditional instruments. The dancers also participated in student and faculty seminars and visited classes on campus. This exchange expanded our cultural horizons and set the tone for making greater progress in building community at Union College. Nevertheless, in some cases over the last 30 years, the college administration has lacked the resources (and possibly the resolve) to consistently identify the perpetrators of insensitivity towards members of marginalized groups on campus. As a result, some constituencies on campus have felt from time to time that there has been a lack of accountability for promoting a campus environment that is intolerant of bigotry in all of its forms.

A sign of my hope for a Union that embraces and celebrates diversity is its dramatic change since I joined the faculty in 1965. A quick look at the students pictured in the yearbooks after that year affirms Union's trend toward inclusivity and away from exclusivity. In 1965, Union was not open to women students, but in 1970 the college enrolled its first women. Since then, the college has improved its efforts to encourage diversity, but some events at Union are poorly attended by students. These are learning opportunities that expand a student's horizons beyond the confines of academic subjects and contribute to the development of a well-rounded person.

Carl and I established Unitas to celebrate diversity and encourage understanding amongst all members of the Union community. Unitas strives to raise awareness of and provide insight into and respect for our differences while also celebrating our common humanity. We are all brothers and sisters! Unitas presents two annual awards: One to the college senior who has done the most to promote diversity on campus; the second to a member of the faculty, staff, or student body who has done the most to contribute to community building.

Since its founding, Unitas has contributed over $103,000 to promote community and diversity on campus. In fact, in 2000, an award of $5,000 was *offered* to any faculty member that wished to formulate a proposal to bring the campus community closer together. To our disappointment, there were no faculty who submitted proposals for this award.

Union College president Stephen Ainlay and his wife, Judith, supported Unitas and provided the visionary leadership to ensure that our students have the opportunities and resources to prepare them for life, work, and success in a diverse and global society.

A MORE FORMAL TIME

My mind sometimes drifts back to the first faculty reception I attended in 1965. It was bound by long-time protocol and tradition, and held in Alumni Gym. Women dressed in their finest evening wear and jewelry, and men were attired in tuxedos. It was the first time that senior faculty had the opportunity to check out the newcomers, and one had to be on his or her best behavior. It was a "get to know you" event, and a time when senior faculty members caught up on summer activities. I felt like I was under a microscope.

Club life was important on campus at that time. The Minerva Club, a club for the wives of faculty members, met periodically for tea and crafts and square-dancing. Twice a month, a member of the faculty hosted interested dancers in his home. A professor of physics led the group and was a strict disciplinarian. When people made a misstep and turned the wrong way, he promptly corrected them.

There was another challenge to being the new kid on the block: I could not park behind the biology building. There were three parking spots, and they were reserved for the biology department chairman and two senior faculty members. Union was no exception to seniority-based perks and privileges. Now that I am retired, I enjoy the honors and privileges that come with being Professor Emeritus. I have been granted an office with a desk and computer, and can park as close to campus buildings as I wish to!

CONTINUING EDUCATION
AND PROFESSIONAL CONTRIBUTIONS

What was continuing education like at Union? Well, it was important for me as well as for my students. I tried to go to every conference, every seminar, and every professional development meeting that was possible for me to attend. Brief examples of my enthusiasm for continuing education include participating in a collaborative learning workshop in 1993, attending a conference on AIDS at Temple University in 1992, and enrolling in a short immunology course at Albany Medical College in 1981. Moreover, in the late 1980s, I spent a day at the Austin Jones Science Tissue College located in Saranac Lake, New York, and took a field trip there with my students studying immunology the following year. Later that same year, I also took a two-day course in advanced immunology at Hampshire College in Massachusetts. During the summer of 1985, I traveled to Vanderbilt University to take a week-long course in electron histochemistry, and I later spent three days at Northeastern University studying electron microscopy.

In 1989, I spent my summer at the University of Wisconsin learning about governance and administrative advancement. I never focused on climbing the administrative ladder, however. I simply wanted to have better insight into what administrators do. Just like in the Army, it is vital to know the chain of command and how authority and responsivity intersect to accomplish administrative goals.

My 1963 doctoral dissertation was on the effect of bacterial endotoxins on *Trypanosoma lewisi (T. lewisi)* infection in rats. I discovered that the longer rats were exposed to endotoxins, the more resistant to parasites they became. As a result of this initial study, the research interests I pursued at Union College primarily focused on the immunological features of parasitic infections in laboratory animal models. I performed research on the effects of malaria on mice and continued my work on *T. lewisi* infections in rats.

In addition to this work, I did collaborative research with Dr. Ellis Lee at General Electric in Schenectady and Dr. Kenneth Amiraian, an immuno-chemist at the New York State Department of Health's Wadsworth Center in Albany. During the academic year, I spent part of my time at Union researching the effect of high-density lipoproteins on *T. Lewisi*. Dr. Amiraian also spent part of his year coming over to Union College to do research with me. This partnership worked well, and we were able to publish our work in peer-reviewed journals.

One professional highlight I'd like to mention is my delivering a paper in Beijing, China, in 1988. My wife, Connie, and I were invited to go on a People to People Tour of China, and during our two-week visit to Beijing, Xiamen, Xian, Chongqing, Shanghai, and Hong Kong we both delivered papers in our respective fields. I remember giving a talk to doctors and staff members at a Chinese hospital in Beijing titled, "The Lytic Activity of Rat High Density Lipoproteins Against *Trypanosoma lewisi* in vitro." Being in China at that time was eye-opening, and although it was very traditional and conservative society, I could see that it had the potential to change culturally and economically. Lo and behold, it has!

Going back in time a bit, in 1981, I delivered a research paper at the Society of Protozoology Annual Meeting in Dallas titled, "Teaching Protozoology at Union College." That same year, I served on the education committee of the Society of Protozoology, too. Also in 1981, I accompanied Connie to several medical conferences that she attended as a physician specializing in the field of pediatrics. The lectures and discussions she attended focused on topics that I was also interested in such as emerging concepts in genetics, physiology, cell biology, and immunology, and in viral, bacterial, and parasitic infectious diseases. In ensuing years, I often incorporated what I learned from her conferences into the lectures I gave to my own students.

Almost thirty years after earning my Ph.D. at NYU, I was invited to be the first Summer-in-Residence Research Scholar in the Faculty Resource Network at NYU. I then stayed on to work for a year (1991-1992) at the NYU Medical School's Department of Molecular Parasitology with Dr. Alan Clarkson, conducting research on the cultivation of *Pneumocystis carinii*, the opportunistic infectious agent prevalent in patients with HIV/AIDS. Later that year, I was selected to go to Dillard University in New Orleans for three days to help them revise their biology curriculum and give a seminar on HIV/AIDs. In 1981, I founded the AIDS Committee at Union College, and in 1982, Professor Karen Williams joined me as a co-chair of the AIDS Committee. She worked so diligently on the one-week conferences we held at Union during every academic year until 1990. We feel that we impacted people's lives because we provided them with current information to change and possibly save their lives. We also appreciated the support we received from the New York State Department of Health, the Schenectady Health Department, and the many colleges and universities in the Capital District area. As a result of our collective efforts, Union College was at the vanguard of educating the Capital District about all issues surrounding the AIDS epidemic.

Last, when I transitioned from full Professor of Biology to emeritus status in 1997, I had the opportunity to complete the education that I had missed during my youth and undergraduate years. I mentioned earlier in this work that Virginia Union did not offer many electives in the 1940s: it offered no courses in music or the arts.

So, from 1997 to 2007, my colleagues at Union granted me permission to audit courses in humanities that I never had the opportunity to take while in college. I took three courses in political science from Professor Clifford Brown, Jr., three from Professor Lorraine Cox and Louisa Matthews in art history, one from Professor Martin Benjamin in photography, and one from Professor Linda Patrick in philosophy. My most challenging course was offered by Professor Diane McMullen, who taught me about music from the Medieval period to the present.

I'll never forget the three courses I took from music professor Tim Olsen, however. As it turned out, three of my biology colleagues were also auditing his course on Latin American music, but I was one of few who volunteered to take the tests and final exam for it. After I completed it, I thought I had done very well, but when he returned my paper, I saw that it was marked with a "90." I asked him what had happened, and he replied, "You left out a 10-point question. Better luck next time!" I had to laugh. I guess my memory was good enough to answer the questions but not good enough to remember to complete them all!

Auditing these courses brought me great deal of fulfillment. I bought all the books for and studied hard in all of them. I began my studies at 70 years old and stretched my neurons until they reached 80. Who says age is a barrier to learning? After all this effort, I felt that I had finally started to be an intellectual, not just a specialist in one field. Take it from me: Every-one can be a life-long learner!

STUDY TOUR

In the late 1990s, Dr. Martha Huggins, a professor of sociology at Union College, invited Connie and I and other professors to join the travel portion of the last three weeks of her ten-week course in Brazil. Her students would continue to live with their host families, and we adults would stay in hotels. Before we left the States, she sent all of us a syllabus with articles about the sociological, political, and cultural challenges faced by Brazilians. After we arrived, she and her colleague, Professor Malcolm Willison (a professor of sociology, as well, at Union) gave us handouts to be read before the end of each day. They did a great job of organizing and coordinating our activities.

Our first extracurricular activity was attending Brazilian Samba schools (small institutions that would teach and prepare community groups all year to compete in the annual Carnival). We toured one school and marveled at the numerous trophies that had been won over the years by several families. Preparing for Carnival (the annual festival held between the Friday before Ash Wednesday until Ash Wednesday, the beginning of Lent) is a very serious endeavor that builds pride and community in Brazil.

Our second activity was visiting Sao Paulo, a city with deep Japanese heritage. Most people don't know that Brazil is home to more people of Japanese descent than any country outside of Japan. The first sizable population of Japanese came to Brazil in 1908 because of a shortage in Italian workers on Brazilian coffee plantations and because of economic difficulties in some areas of rural Japan.

After a few days of exploring the tourist attractions of Sao Paulo, we boarded a plane en route to the Pantanal (in English, the "Great Swamp"), particularly the Campo Grande region in the state of Mato Grasso. Located in central-eastern Brazil, it is one of the most important ecosystems in the world, an enormous plain that is bisected by the Paraguay River and its tributaries. Thousands of exotic plants and animal species make it their home, and it is located approximately 500 miles south of the Amazon Jungle. Belying its name, the Pantanal is not a swamp but a salubrious region rich in flora and fauna—a biologist's dream! Moreover, we were there during the latter part of November and were quite fortunate that the heavy rains, which usually occur from October until March, had not flooded the expansive plain. As we travelled by van through the country to our camp site, we could see many farms with herds of cattle, wild animals, and exotic vegetation. We were awestruck by the capybaras and caimans, and the deer, anteaters, armadillos, tapirs, otters, and anacondas in the forests.

Our typical day would be leaving our camp early in the morning for field studies in an open truck with two benches that seated twelve people. Occasionally, we had to get out of the open-air truck and push it because we were stuck in the mud. Because all of the roads had ruts, holes, and ditches, we would bounce up and down like a basketball. On our way to our morning destinations, we would see many ponds with colorful giant water lilies, short trees, brush, and other foliage. Open tracts of land were abundant, and we could see for miles.

I remember one day when we arrived at our field site, we noticed that the small river nearby contained piranhas, and that twenty hungry caimans—at least ten-feet long—basked along the riverbank patiently waiting for prey. Under the supervision of our guides, some of our brave male students used a long pole with meat to entice them to climb up the bank and greet us, but the caimans wouldn't budge, much to our relief! That evening, after we had finished discussing what we had seen, we went outside our large tent, looked up at the sky, and it was charcoal black. What a glorious site! With no electric lights in sight, the stars were glistening like sparkling diamonds. I could have watched the heavens until dawn, but we all had to attend classes the next day. When we left the Pantanal, we flew to Brasilia, Bahia, Rio de Janeiro, and then home. These cities were more for tourists—interesting but not as spectacular as the Pantanal.

Over my career, I have found that terms abroad are one of the most enriching experiences an adult or student can experience. I was fortunate to have worked with Martha years before on a course in Bogota, Colombia, so I was one of the first professors she asked to accompany the students to Brazil. It was an experience of a lifetime, and I am forever grateful to her for inviting Connie and me to join her group.

COMMUNITY SERVICE

Along with teaching, research, and college service, Union College also expected its teachers to perform community service. I developed a strong commitment to community service when I joined the faculty in 1965. My early
community service activities included board membership of public television station WMHT, the Mohawk Council of Educational Television, and
Channel 17 (a television channel that focused on local news from the Capital
District), respectively, from 1968 to 1974, and for a second term from 1977
to 1985. I also served as its secretary when the station was first founded.

During this same time period, I served on the citizen advisory committee for the Capital District Regional Planning Commission, and on the
Board of Trustees of the Southern Adirondack chapter of the National
Foundation for Birth Defects. At this time, the March of Dimes played a
critical role in raising funds for handicapped children who had polio. To
my great delight, I had the opportunity to meet Dr. Jonas Salk—inventor
of the polio vaccine—and travelled to La Jolla, California, to have lunch
with him and other members of his research team. Moreover, I served on
the Board of Trustees for the Saratoga United Way, the Board of Trustees
for the Schenectady County Cancer Society, the Board of Trustees for the
Schenectady County Mental Health Association, and the Board of the Al-

cohol Counsel for Schenectady County. I also served on the first committee for Schenectady County Planned Parenthood from 1966-1969. In addition, I was one of the original founders of the Southern Saratoga County YMCA, which eventually built a separate branch in our hometown of Clifton Park.

Over the years, I've also been a member of the Board of the Library Association of Clifton Park, and have served on the board of the Carver Community Center, an organization founded to serve the educational and recreational needs of lower income families in Schenectady. Furthermore, I've served on the board of the Hamilton Hill Arts Center, a place where young African-American artists can go to develop their skills and showcase their art work. The efforts of this organization have provided many opportunities for youth of color to channel their energy and creativity in positive ways instead of in mischief on the streets.

Moreover, I have served as a member of the Business Board of Trustees for Bellevue Maternity Hospital, and witnessed, firsthand, the complex decision-making processes required to deliver quality healthcare. I learned about the hospital's challenges with staffing nurses and doctors, and with providing patients and practitioners with the latest equipment and facilities in the face of ever-present budgetary constraints. I can say with conviction that we always did our best to ensure that the hospital provided the best possible care for pregnant women.

Dr. Grace Jorgensen's mother was the founder and original owner of Bellevue Maternity Hospital. Members of its board were invited to attend healthcare-related meetings in various parts of the United States, and as a result I traveled to San Francisco, New Orleans, Orlando, Washington, D.C., and New York City, amongst many other cities. During one of these trips, I was fortunate to meet former U.S. Senator Robert Dole who served in WWII and sustained serious injuries to his right arm. Many years later when I traveled to Washington, D.C., as part of the Leather Stocking Honor

Flight for veterans of WWII and the Korean War, Senator Dole, whom I had met thirty years prior, greeted our group. I kidded him when I asked, "Do you and your wife remember me?" He replied, "Of course!" kidding me back. He then took a photograph with me. What a great experience this was for me! Senator Dole is a nice man and a true patriot.

With regard to my other community service activities, I was host and assistant planner of one of the 21st Annual Meetings of the American Society of Microbiologists held at Lake George, New York, in the 1990s. I have also served on the animal welfare committee for Wadsworth Laboratories at the New York State Department of Health, and have been a member of the board of the Bridge Center of Schenectady for about eight or nine years, a center that helps men and women drug addicts recover and return to society as productive members. I found working on this board to be challenging but also very rewarding. I've also been on the Diversity Committees for the Schenectady Museum, the Southern Saratoga YMCA, the Capital District Regional Planning Committee, and Sigma Pi Phi fraternity. At present, I'm a member of the Scotia Rotary Club, and have been recognized as a Paul Mellon Fellow of the club.

Furthermore, at various times during my career at Union, I have served on the Admissions Committee, the Graduate Studies Committee, the Lectures and Concert Committee, the College Discipline Committee, the Minority Affairs Committee, the Outward-Bound Committee, the Health-Related Profession Committee, and the Library Committee. I also served on either the tenure or professional review committees for three faculty members and one staff member: Drs. Kenneth De Bono, Assistant Professor of Psychology (1991); Judith Ginsberg, Assistant Professor of Spanish in the department of foreign languages (1980); John Boyd, Assistant Professor of Biological Sciences (one of my colleagues); and Janet Gregory, a government documents specialist in the

Union College library. For many years, I was also a faculty advisor for freshman orientation.

In addition, I was a member of Union's Pre-Medical Advising Committee for more than twenty-five years. My colleagues and I advised, screened, and wrote recommendations for students seeking admission to medical school and health-related professions. We met on Fridays from 1:00 p.m. until 4:00 p.m. There were eight of us on the committee, and we spent hours discussing and vetting each candidate. The pre-medical students had no idea that so much time and effort took place to help them be admitted to their desired medical schools.

I was also fortunate to be able to take several sabbatical leaves: one at the University of Veterinary Medicine in Guelph, Ontario, and another at New York University in Manhattan. Moreover, I served the larger academic community as a member of the Middle States Association evaluation team, which is part of the larger Commission on the Higher Education of Colleges and Universities. Members of these evaluation teams reviewed the quality of educational research provided by Mid-Atlantic colleges and universities, and my specific team focused on the performance of biology departments in this region.

I have contributed to the accreditation reviews for the biology departments: Gettysburg College in Pennsylvania; Fairleigh Dickinson University in Teaneck, New Jersey; the University of Maryland—Eastern Shore in Princess Anne, Maryland; Stockton State College in Pomona, New Jersey; The University of the District of Columbia in Washington, D.C.; Saint Vincent College in Latrobe, Pennsylvania; St. Francis University in Loretto, Pennsylvania; Delvalle College in Buffalo, New York; Inter-American College in San Juan, Puerto Rico; and Le Moyne College in Syracuse, New York. To me, one university stood out among the many we evaluated: Carnegie Mellon University. Its facilities, curriculum, and goals and objectives stood far above the others. I believe that its strong endowment was a major factor that drove its excellence. Nevertheless, I came to realize over the years that Union College was also in the vanguard compared to other smaller institutions. It stood out in terms of the quality of its students, faculty, and curriculum. The opportunity for students to do independent research, and the quality of the rapport between students and faculty at Union was extraordinary.

Union College faculty are expected to conduct research and engage in scholarship as well. One special opportunity for me to do so was when I was selected as The Jesse Ball DuPont fellow and scholar at Marymount University in Arlington, Virginia. My duties during this one-year appointment included revising and reviewing the biology curriculum and teaching one course each semester. I worked closely with faculty, students and staff at Marymount, and taught immunology and parasitology courses. Having spent my entire career at secular Union College, teaching at a Catholic institution was an eye-opening experience for me. The biggest difference I immediately observed was that there was more order. Like Union, but in contrast to some secular colleges, expectations were very high in terms of teaching and research responsibilities. Faculty members were also required to attend chapel once a week. Whenever the college held all-faculty conferences and meetings, all of the faculty had to be present. If they did not or could not attend, they would have to make up the missed time on another day. Marymount's culture was very rigid.

On the other hand, the students with whom I interacted were calm, respectful, and serious. They didn't cut across the lawns of the campus but would always use the sidewalks. It was a great experience. I reconnected with the advantages that a disciplined college culture could provide. While not at the level of my military experience, the order and structure at Marymount were refreshing, bringing me back to the time when I served in the U.S. Army.

MY CLASSMATES

In my graduating class of 1948 at Virginia Union University, there were three students who eventually became medical doctors but whose first names I don't recall. I do know that their surnames were Bowles, Sutton, and Brown. Another outstanding alumnus in my class was Vice-Admiral Samuel L. Gravely. He was the first African-American commissioned through the Naval Reserve Training Corps to reach flag rank and to command a fleet. While he was on shore leave from his first ship, he was arrested for impersonating an officer: "You are not an officer," he was told by a military policeman who also said to him, "I've never seen a Negro naval officer." Despite this kind of treatment, he rose to Vice Admiralship and in 2010 had a new destroyer commissioned in his name: the *USS Gravely (DDG-107)*.

In the late 1990s, Auria and I were invited to and attended a reception in his honor at the Naval Command Station in Washington, D.C., before he retired. He is now deceased. Another classmate, Mrs. Evelyn Syphax, who did well in business, donated one million dollars to VUU. Later, VUU decided to name a building in her honor. The lesson here is that historically black colleges and universities (HBCUs) can produce outstanding and successful Americans just like traditionally white colleges and universities can.

OUR CHILDREN'S EDUCATION

Like my father, Peter, I believe that education is the "north star" to a better life. My wife, Connie, shared with me the same belief, and we spared no effort to support the education of our two children. Homework was checked, parent-teacher conferences were faithfully attended, PTA meetings were participated in, and we followed all the activities at our children's schools. We volunteered whenever and wherever we could, and supported them in any way we could.

Moreover, Connie and I mentored our children at all stages. I recall a guidance counselor advising our son, Scott, "Don't apply to Ivy League schools because you will not get in." He gave Scott this advice notwithstanding grades that placed Scott in the top 3% of his high school graduating class of about 650 students, and merited his placement in the National Honor Society. Undeterred, both Scott and Auria applied to Ivy League schools, were accepted at all the ones they applied to, and they both chose Princeton. They both had a terrific educational experience at Princeton, and have held several interesting jobs in their careers: currently, Scott is a teacher, coach, and adviser at a boarding school in New Hampshire, and Auria is an in-house corporate attorney in California.

I firmly believe all parents should be fully invested in the education of their children. I didn't have to go to their school often to ensure that they were being treated fairly, but they knew that I was there to watch over them. When they went to Princeton, I told them if the professors did not respond to their questions or provide them with help when they asked, they should let me know.

Fortunately, Princeton is one of the best teaching institutions in the world. However, one incident that was less than pleasant comes to mind. One summer, our tuition check did not arrive until August 17, 1987, but was due on August 15, 1987. Classes started on September 15, 1987. They charged me a $50 late fee. I spoke to the bursar about it, but he did not remove the fee. I paid the fine, but told him emphatically over the phone, "You are thieves!" and never to write me again for a donation. I also said, "If you want any more donations, ask my children." They took me off their solicitation list, and I never gave them another penny. I have not heard from Princeton since, and I am glad. Can you imagine a school with billions of dollars in endowment funds treating a parent with two children at their institution like that? Wow! To me, this was an unforgettable and unpardonable event. Princeton is the school my children graduated from, but I don't hold its blind adherence to policy in high esteem: As a son of Prince Edward County, their inflexibility reminded me of the "Massive Resistance" to integration and of the all-white colleges and universities that were closed to a person of color like me.

ROBERT RUSSA MOTON MUSEUM—PART TWO

It is interesting how life experiences are tied together. The Martha E. Forrester Council of Colored Women, founded by a woman I knew as a boy, was organized in 1920 to improve schools and make Farmville a more inclusive and welcoming place. Despite all the mean, hateful, and oppressive acts many town citizens committed, something good came out of closing R.R. Moton, the school that I attended and later taught at. After the school was closed, the county decided to build the new Prince Edward County Schools on Rt. 15S, a few miles south of town on the road to Hampden Sydney College. Black students were not allowed to attend them from 1959-1964, but thereafter they could.

The original building of the school I attended and taught at was left to deteriorate and fall apart, its roof was leaking, and there were several physical plant problems. The building was going to be demolished until the Martha E. Forrester Council of Colored Women decided in the late 1990s to purchase it and preserve it for historical reasons. The foresight and dedication of this organization to educating people about Farmville's history attests to their commitment to preserving its legacy and importance.

Robert Russa Moton was born on August 26, 1867, in Amelia County, Virginia, was raised in Prince Edward County, and later became an administrator at Hampton University. He later became the principal of Tuskegee Institute. These two institutions of higher learning are classified as Historically Black Colleges and Universities (HBCUs), most of which were established after the Civil War with the intention of serving the black community.

Today, the old Robert Russa Moton High School has been turned into a museum to chronicle the civil rights events that occurred there from 1951 to 1964, particularly the 1951 Moton School student strike against separate and unequal educational facilities and resources. In recent years, the museum has been designated as a National Historic Landmark, and is located on Griffin Boulevard, the street that I lived on (it was formerly called Ely Street) when my dad moved us from Five Forks to Farmville in the early 1930s. The museum is considered by many to be "the student birthplace of America's Civil Rights Movement," and is on the registry of U.S. National Historic Places and on the Registry of Virginia Landmarks.

In 2013, the museum's first permanent exhibition was opened to the public, and was titled, "The Moton School Story: Children of Courage." It has attracted thousands of visitors from all over the world, including students and educators eager to learn more about the museum's past, present, and future.

In March 2017, I was invited to attend and be a guest speaker at the Sixth Annual Moton Community Banquet held on the campus of Longwood University. The keynote speaker was Anne Holton, former Secretary of Education for the State of Virginia and the wife of Senator Tim Kane, Hillary Clinton's running mate for Vice President of the United States. Her father, Linwood Holton, served as Virginia's governor from 1970-1974, and she and her family helped to integrate Richmond's schools during her father's term.

The banquet was sold out. The crowning event for the evening was a presentation made by the Honorable Mark Peake, a Virginia State Senator.

He read Joint Senate Resolution #30 designating April 21st in 2018, and in each succeeding year, as "Barbara Johns Day" in Virginia. Later in the evening, my wife and I received the Family Challenge Award for donating $25,000 to the Moton Museum. This fall, two students from PEC will be attending college because so many friends, educators, and businessmen donated to the Moton Museum. Our gift will ensure that the Styles Family name is associated with the Moton Museum and with Farmville's civil rights struggle well into the future. Twenty members of my family attended this historic event, and Anne Hammond, the daughter of Dorothy Vaughan—the main character of the movie, *Hidden Figures*, and also my high school mathematics teacher—came as our guest.

TRAVELS

During my educational career, I was blessed and awarded with many scholarships and fellowships to further my education and to conduct research on tropical diseases the eradication of which would improve the quality of life in America and throughout the world. Many of these opportunities allowed me to travel internationally, which also satisfied my insatiable appetite for learning about new countries and cultures.

One day in March of 1998, Auria called from Hong Kong and said that she was going to go on a three-week trip to Southeast Asia during the upcoming summer. She planned to go to Thailand, Malaysia, Singapore, and Bali. I told her I would arrange to meet her at the airport in Hong Kong and then we could fly to Thailand.

Thailand

Upon arrival in Hong Kong, Auria boarded the same plane I was on, and we together flew to Bangkok. As we deplaned in Bangkok, there was a driver holding a sign that said, "Prof. Styles." A former student of mine named Lina and her mother had sent their Mercedes to transport us to our hotel. When we arrived at our hotel, other people on our trip looked at us and wondered, "Who are these folks?" We spent about five days there and were treated like royalty by Lina's family. They arranged for us to go to the Royal Summer Palace by car and chauffeur, and took us on a personal tour of Bangkok. We remember going to many Buddhist temples where we had to take off our shoes and leave them outside. The temples reminded me of scenes from the Broadway production, *The King and I* (1951) based on the relationship that Anglo-Indian travel writer, educator, and social activist Anna Leonowens and the King of Siam had in the 1860s. Moreover, each evening, they took us out for fine dining, and the food was out of this world. Lina's mother owned three jewelry shops, and before we left, she invited us to visit each one. We went and sat down before a counter looking at the elegant jewelry for sale. A clerk soon came over and brought us tea and cookies as we perused the gemstones. I purchased a small gift for all members of my immediate family. I knew that we were getting an excellent price that others would not find anywhere else in town. It was a first-class shop.

The night before we left, we had an opportunity to visit the Patpong district, an internationally known shopping and red light district in the heart of Bangkok. There, people can find exotic night life, go-go girls, massage parlors, prostitutes, bars, and adult shows in many buildings in the area. Our escort to Patpong invited me to go to the second floor of one of the venues, and I noticed scantily clad ladies dancing, gyrating, and enticing patrons to spend money on them. Auria was downstairs where there were open air markets and vendors selling fake brand name goods (e.g., Fendi, Prada, Gucci, Izod, and Perry Ellis). She did not buy anything, and after a short time, ran upstairs and said, "Daddy, I am going to tell Mom." I must admit, the activities upstairs were sights to behold! The last night we were there, we had a sumptuous dinner with Lina's entire family that we all enjoyed very much.

The next leg of our visit to Thailand took us north on a one-hour flight. The plane seated 300 passengers and was full. In 90 minutes, we were on the ground in Chang Mai, the largest city in northern Thailand and the capital of the Lan Na Kingdom from 1296 to 1768. Elephants are important to the culture of Thailand, and it was in Chang Mai that we had an opportunity to visit an elephant park. What an experience! The elephants were well trained and appeared to be calm, happy, well-cared for, and obedient. We watched them feeding and taking their morning showers in the river, and took advantage of the opportunity to ride them bareback. Riding atop such a large and majestic creature took a bit of getting used to, but little by little, I settled in, and my fear diminished. This was one of the highlights of our trip to Thailand.

Singapore

We then journeyed from Thailand to Singapore, and upon arrival, Auria and I were met by two of her former classmates at Princeton. They greeted us warmly and took us to view the botanic gardens. The gardens housed some of the world's most exotic orchids and other flora—beautiful sights to behold and not to be forgotten! Auria and I took a guided tour of the city, and also attended an exhibit of Andy Warhol's art at the Singapore Museum. In contrast to some of the other cities and countries we visited during our travels, we had few, if any, concerns regarding our safety while in Singapore.

Malaysia

After leaving Singapore, our next destination was Malaysia. There we were met by a friend who had been an American Field Service (AFS) student for a summer and lived with our neighbor in Clifton Park. She spent time taking us to museums, mosques, and tourist attractions. Our fellow travelers were surprised to see that we had such a connection so far away from us in the States. I'm sure that they were thinking, "How do they know so many folks out here in Asia?" Throughout the tour, we were reconnecting with friends who had returned home to their native countries after spending time living in the U.S.

We then visited the Petronas Twin Towers in Kuala Lumpur, the tallest buildings in the world from 1998-2004. They feature a double sky bridge connecting the 41st and 42nd floors, and remain a key tourist attraction in Malaysia. After living for ten years in NYC, I thought I was used to being impressed by tall buildings. However, the sight of the Petronas Towers dominating the skyline of Kuala Lumpur truly impressed me.

BELGIUM, DEAR FRIENDS AND A LIBRARY

My family and I hosted an AFS student from Belgium named Marleen Platteborze during the summer of 1990. While living with us, she participated in activities typical for high school students, and demonstrated a keen interest in art and painting. Moreover, she was very intellectual, and took many summer courses. The following year, our daughter, Auria, was invited by Marleen's family to spend a summer with them. At the end of Auria's summer in Belgium, my wife and I traveled there to visit Marleen and her family. We met her dad, mother, and sister Katrien. We stayed with them for one week, and they took us to visit many tourist attractions in Bruges, Kent, Antwerp, Germany, and Lichtenstein. We saw paintings by Rubens and other "Old World" masters.

When we dined out, we often drank Belgian beer, and ate delicious Belgian mussels and waffles. The Platteborze family's home is located about five miles from Brussels in a town named Korbeek-Lo, with a population of about 2,000 (about half the population of Farmville, Virginia, in the 1930s).

One day, my wife Connie and I were confused when Marleen's parents, William (Wim) and Annie Platteborze, said that they wanted us to see something that would have special significance for us. We couldn't imagine what it was. It turned out to be the Leuven (also known as "Louvain") University library, which was originally built in 1425. Only a ten-minute drive from their home, William drove us from Korbeek-Lo to the campus of Leuven University. As we approached by car, an imposing building came into view. It was a designed by American architect Whitney Warren (1864-1943) in the style known as the "Neo-Renaissance of the Low Countries." Mr. Warren also contributed to the architectural designs of Grand Central Terminal and the Biltmore Hotel in New York City.

In August of 1914, German troops set fire to the library and much of the city of Leuven. The library's collection of more than 300,000 books, an untold number of rare manuscripts, and irreplaceable medieval and renaissance treasures were burned to ashes. This barbarous destruction aroused international indignation, and before WWI ended, committees were formed in allied and neutral countries to collect books and money to fund the reconstruction of the Leuven University library. The library is located on Ladeuzeplein Square (on the campus of the university), and took eight years to complete its post-war reconstruction. The library is stunning from the outside and even more impressive inside. The world celebrated is reopening in 1928. Nicholas Murray Butler (1862-1947) was the chair of the National Committee of the United States for the Restoration of the University of Leuven and later chair of the Carnegie Endowment for International Peace. In 1931, he was awarded the Nobel Peace Prize for his leadership in strengthening international law and the International Court at the Hague.

From the outset, the building was meant to be reconstructed as a Belgian national monument and has been classified as such since 1987. The interior of the building is rich in great war iconography. Homage is also paid to Belgian luminaries including Cardinal Mercier, King Albert I, and Queen Elizabeth. One-hundred thirty-six engraved stones, an American eagle, and 48 stars on the side of the building honor the role American citizens played in its rebuilding and restoration. Commemorative stones came from colleges, high schools, and donors from around the world. To our surprise, William brought us to a commemorative stone in the wall memorializing a donation from Union College, my employer for over 30 years. My interest in finding out more about Union's gift to the library was thus piqued: Over the years, I have been trying to obtain more information about when and how much money Union gave to the library's reconstruction. I have since talked with the Leuven University library archivist to see if he had information in the archives concerning Union's donation but he didn't. He told me that any such record would have been destroyed in 1940 by Nazi invaders under Hitler. I also checked Union College's archives, the records maintained by Schenectady's *Daily Gazette* newspaper, and the Schenectady Historical Society but all came up empty. I am not sure that many members of the Union College family are aware of Union's gift to this library in Leuven, Belgium. For as long as I am able to, I will spread this news.

Wim and Annie Platteborze are part of our family. They and their children mean so much to us. He is also the designer of the cover of this book: *Son of Prince Edward County.*

SAFARI

In May of 1996, Scott called me from Princeton and asked if I would like to travel with him to South Africa in August. I initially and emphatically said, "No," but in retrospect can't remember why—perhaps because of the distance and the time it would take to get there. Scott and two of his colleagues had been selected by their graduate school advisor to present papers on their research at the Fifth Biennial Conference of the International Network of Philosophers of Education held at Rand Afrikaans University in Johannesburg (Jo'burg), South Africa. I had no intentions of changing my mind but Scott was persistent, and after several calls, I decided to go. The night before we left on our 20-hour trip, we took the subway from Queens to Manhattan to see *Sunset Boulevard*, a hit musical that was receiving rave reviews on Broadway at the time. The following morning, we boarded our flight from JFK Airport to London's Heathrow, and waited three hours for our 11-hour nonstop flight to Johannesburg.

Upon arrival, we were met by the brother of one of Scott's classmates (a white South African) at Princeton who took us to a nice bed and breakfast in the suburbs and while there gave us well-informed tours of Jo'burg and its environs. The fact that we were in South Africa only three years after Nelson Mandela had been released from prison was not lost on me, so I was sensitive to how Scott and I would be treated by the white South Africans while we were there. It didn't take long to find out because the next day we went to the university, were told where Scott would give his talk, and were given instructions on how to use the audio-visual equipment in the lecture room. As we passed through the halls, many of the white students looked straight ahead, not making eye contact, as though we were invisible. Their body language, too, was off-putting and screamed, "Get out of here! Go back to where you're from...where there's tolerance of ethnic and racial differences." Fortunately, we anticipated such behavior and didn't give it a second thought.

Scott's seminar presentation went very well and many students and faculty in the audience asked questions of him. An African-American alumna of Princeton whom Scott had contacted prior to leaving the States was in the audience, and she congratulated and thanked him, and invited us to meet her later in the evening at a jazz club that she frequented with friends. She picked us up, paid the parking attendant the fee and then paid another "attendant" to watch her car and protect it from vandalism, a big problem both then and now in Jo'burg. She parked her car and we went into the club where people were sitting at tables arranged cabaret style and ordered some drinks, and then some appetizers. I recall her ordering for us the following: grilled springbok (a cousin of the antelope), biltong (meat jerky), stewed ostrich, grilled boerewors (lamb and pork sausage), and my favorite, mopani worms (fried moth caterpillars) with fruit chutney. To say South Africa was a culinary adventure was an understatement—we've never had such exotic foods since!

After listening to cool jazz and feasting on our appetizers, we returned to the parking lot but were shocked when we noticed the driver's side window smashed and the radio stolen. Some "attendant!" Scott's friend then called her brother who called the South African equivalent of AAA, and then he picked us up in his own car. Throughout the ordeal, she remained calm and poised. She said that petty crime was rampant at the time, and that it "happens to everyone."

After four days, Scott's conference concluded, and so we decided to go on a safari to the Kruger National Park, and had the thrill of a lifetime. We were there for four days and three nights, one of which included a night safari in the *veld* (Afrikaans for "open field and grassland"). I'll never forget hearing the shrill cries and seeing the small eyes of the African bushbabies (the smallest primates in Africa) that lived in the trees of the forests. I'll also never forget seeing live and in person the lions, rhinos, hippos, zebra, giraffes, elephants, leopards, and buffalo in their native habitats. Breathtaking.

We also took advantage of the opportunity to visit Soweto, a township in Jo'burg that was the site of the June 16, 1976, Soweto uprising against apartheid. On that day, Afrikaner police opened fire on a group of unarmed student protesters who opposed the mandatory teaching of both Afrikaans and English in the black schools in Soweto. We toured a small museum housed in corrugated tin shacks that depicted the story of the 176 (and, unofficially, three times more) students who died that day while protesting being required to learn the language of their oppressors. I recall being emotionally shaken both my memories of having to attend underprivileged and unequal schools in PEC, and by Scott's face after he emerged from the museum. I had never before seen him so overwhelmed with emotion. After we collected ourselves, I remember asking our tour guide where we could go to have a stiff drink, and she gave us each a big hug and obliged my request.

The rest of the trip was memorable for going to the wine country in Stellenbosch and shipping some unique vintages back to Clifton Park, and for browsing the local sculpture markets. I remember being so fascinated by the quality of the wooden and stone carvings that I took picture after picture so that I could show my friends when we returned.

And, last, I'll never forget running into one of my Union College colleagues at Kirstenbosch National Gardens in Cape Town one afternoon. As we were admiring the beautiful proteas and other flora from five of the six biomes found in South Africa, I heard someone say, "Twitty? Twitty? Is that you?" Sure enough, a Union College administrator was also at Kirstenbosch National Gardens on the same day at the same time that Scott and I were, unplanned. We embraced, had a nice conversation, and then went our separate ways. We touched base when we returned to Union and had quite a story to tell about "living in such a small world." Who would think that you could bump into a colleague unintentionally almost 8,000 miles away from home!

CIVIL RIGHTS MOVEMENT

I was so proud to have had the opportunity to visit the Virginia Civil Rights Memorial located at the Virginia Governor's Mansion in Richmond in 2015. It honors and immortalizes Barbara Johns and other students and civil right heroes who fought for desegregation of the public schools in Prince Edward County.

When all of the civil rights history was in the making, I was AWOL (Absent Without Leave), so to speak. I was there in spirit but not in body. In April 1951, I was disembarking at the Port of Yokohama, Japan, on my way to an active duty assignment in Korea. After my discharge from the Army, I took advantage of the G.I. Bill to continue my education: It took 10 years of hard work and study to earn my doctorate.

My roots run deep in the soil and soul of Farmville and Prince Edward County, and I wish I could have been present to contribute to those history-making times. It was not to be, however. I wonder if I had not been drafted into the Army and left Farmville what course my life would have taken. The course of a person's life journey is part fate, part luck, and partly in the hand of God guiding us along the way.

In 1965, I had finished a post-doctoral fellowship in the Department of Human Ecology at the National University of Mexico Medical School.

It is hard to express my feelings about the history that was made in Farmville before I finished my fellowship. My efforts to earn a Ph.D. during the civil rights struggles in Farmville have enabled me to do more now than if I would have been on the firing lines of protest. The PEC civil rights memorial commemorates and immortalizes the role that the county and its young black students, with the support of Rev. Leslie Griffin, Pastor of First Baptist Church in Farmville, played in the battle to end its segregated and unequal public schools. It was because of the decision in *Griffin v. Prince Edward County* passed down by the U.S. Supreme Court in 1964 that every child in the U. S. has a constitutional right to a public education.

RECOGNIZING BLACK SUCCESS

I was a young boy when we moved from Five Forks to Farmville, Virginia. There were many black men and women that I came to know and admire. The community consisted of a class of educated and accomplished blacks who were successful entrepreneurs and respected professionals. There were doctors, nurses, dentists, ministers, undertakers, postal carriers, teachers, and gifted musicians. Despite the racial barriers endured by these people of color, they all excelled in their chosen field. Through their hard work and frugality, it was possible for them to survive and save a small amount of money to secure in their old age a modest amount of financial security. Unlike in white society, however, old money and property were not handed down through generations, and they had little, if any, political power. It was the era of "Jim Crow"—the system of disfranchisement that shut them out of formal power structures. Nonetheless, they found a "work around" to the system: they contributed to uplifting the quality of life for other blacks in the community by giving back what they could.

When we moved to Clifton Park, NY, in 1965, Connie opened her pediatric office in our home because we could not find adequate places to both live and open an office in Schenectady. My wife would have failed had she tried to build a practice in Schenectady at that time. We got lucky in 1965 because one day we were invited by a colleague at SUNY Albany to visit his friends in Clifton Park. Mr. Robert Van Patten said that he would construct anything we wanted. We wanted to have a home with an office for her practice of pediatrics, and he showed us the plan and said, "If you are not pleased with it, you don't have to take it." He shook our hands and started the construction in May of 1965. He and his team completed it in August of 1965.

Furthermore, we were just starting out and had to apply for a mortgage. An employee at Union College had a husband who worked at the Schenectady Trust Bank. He was a manager and knew that I was a professor and my wife a doctor. In spite of this, we were not given an application for the loan. Why? We were blacks and therefore high risks, we were told, but in reality, it was just racism. Nevertheless, we shopped around and finally found a bank that did not take color into consideration. I had saved money in my pension fund while I was working full-time for the State of New York and going to NYU, so I used it for a down payment. I remember what Pa had taught me when I was a child: save your money and don't let anyone piss on you.

We moved into our new home in Clifton Park the first week of September of 1965, and shortly afterwards, Connie opened her five-room office in our home. Patients came from all over the Capital District and other counties to see her. She was the first pediatrician in Clifton Park, and color did not play a role in her serving the area: It was competence that counted. At age 85, Connie still practices medicine. That five-room home office has since grown into a group practice of five doctors and 26 support staff including physician's assistants and nurses. The practice now occupies a large building on Route 146 about two miles away from her original office. The mid-sixties were an exciting time for us: A new house, Connie's practice, my position at Union, and a new baby.

My responsibilities as a professor at Union and Connie's pediatric practice were all consuming. Our "to-do" list grew ever longer as we worked hard to be good parents to our children, care for Connie's elderly parents, and be successful and productive members of our community. We often felt that we under a microscope, however. I quickly learned that our success was based in large measure on how the community viewed us. Over time, we gained the respect of neighbors and coworkers, students and patients, parents and community leaders. Whenever possible, we tried to give back to our community. We were and are a faith-centered couple and believe that each of us has a responsibility to live by the Golden Rule. We hope that our efforts over the years have helped to impact positively the lives of others in our community. We consider ourselves blessed to have known many friends and acquaintances that we love and cherish.

Having been part of the black community in the Capital District of New York, we have experienced a wide variety of attitudes among our people. Some people we have met have felt as though they have "arrived," and have acted smugly towards us and others. Others have been prejudiced against us and other blacks, and have felt that it was their way or no way. Still others have felt adamant about their old family places in the community, and have been prideful and argumentative. Over time, I have tried my best (but have not been perfect) to hear no evil or speak no evil because I never knew who was related to whom, and what the consequences of talking poorly about someone were. Some people were gatekeepers to black social organizations, fraternities, and sororities, and one had to pass their tests. Did you have good character? Where did you come from? What have you done in the community to warrant admitting you to the local black elite? I know of one couple, a dentist and his wife who, as an educator, screened everyone and made sure he or she was worthy of being accepted into the black social circle. Her behavior reminded me of when I was growing up in Farmville and admission into some "bourgeois" black organizations required one to pass the "brown paper" bag test. If your skin was darker than a brown paper bag, some light-skinned blacks would prevent you from joining "their" organizations. To our surprise, when we were in Brazil, we found that color was not as much of a problem as economic status was. We were told by many cab drivers there that money "whitens" you. This phenomenon is true to some extent today in the U.S., but even rich black celebrities like Oprah, Tiger Woods, Beyonce, and Michael Jordan have been subject to racism from time to time.

Today, we might be considered as black middle-class because we are professionals in the Capital District. In the Capital District, lifestyles differ between the "black haves" and the "black have nots." We are referred to as a "power couple." I don't know what that means, but we try to help people because we were taught to reach out to others in need, and we try to never forget the bridges that brought us across.

Moreover, my associates and friends are dedicated to lifting as we climb. It has been said that we were born with two hands: One to take care of ourselves and the other to reach out and help those less fortunate. Many of my friends have graduate degrees, jobs in the New York State Civil Service, in educational institutions, or run their own businesses. They dress well, educate their children, and purchase homes. Many of them support the Carver Community Center, Hamilton Hill Arts Center, Habitat for Humanity, local churches, lodges, food pantries, civil rights organizations, and historically black colleges and universities (HBCUs). They are on the battlefield to make sure that the next generations of children are given an opportunity to succeed by mentoring, teaching, and trying to keep them out of trouble. They also want them to be financially savvy by teaching them how to save money in the bank, to own IRA's, stocks, and bonds, and to collect art and other wealth-building possessions.

I think the reason some of us "fail" is because of a lack of preparation for job opportunities, particularly for those in science, mathematics, and technologies. For blacks to get ahead, we must adopt and incorporate continuing education and not be complacent with a college degree or spending an inordinate amount of time in front of the TV watching sports and reality TV shows hoping that things will change for us. It is so easy for some of us to think, "I have earned my education. I have made it." No! We are just beginning.

On another note, I have had many confrontations in organizations because I am a scientist. I am trained to observe, ask questions, and think things through. My approach to most problems is different from some non-scientists, and some people have been upset with me when I have wanted things explained in a way that is best for all. Moreover, I have been in some organizations in which many people have been reluctant to change anything: once an event has been started, there's been no desire to change anything about it except the date on the program.

I was born in a black world and have had to keep my fundamental values as a God-fearing black person to be able to survive and maneuver in a white one. The key to success for me has been to regard myself as a professional who respects others and expects to be treated in the same way. I have learned how to study body language, speech, and tone, and it does not take me long to get an impression of a person that more often than not proves to be correct. What I do not see in individuals is color. I am trained and programmed to respond to what one says and does—not on what one looks like or believes. I like to say that I have danced with the "devil" when I describe to others all of the conflicts with mean and hateful people I have had. As I traveled my journey and reached the age of 91, I have learned not to let anyone place their stress on me. I like to think that I have a biological defense mechanism that blocks things that might weaken my immune system. In this way, I hope to be stress free for a long time to come.

90TH BIRTHDAY

In January of 2017 (and for many years before), I realized that my 90th birthday was coming soon. My beloved Connie spent several months thinking of how to mark this milestone moment. She decided she would give me a birthday party celebration. In early February of 2017, Connie sent out "save the date" cards that said, "Guess who is turning 90: Twitty Styles." That started a big ball rolling, which involved a lot of scurrying and hurrying to get things done. We wanted our home to be freshly renovated to accommodate our many guests. We surveyed our home inside and outside to determine the changes we would like to implement, and made them. It was exciting to make everything feel fresh and new. It felt as if we had moved into a new home. We hired painters who helped us choose a new color scheme, and contacted a local store to have a representative come to our home and recommend curtains and draperies. We also hired a landscape company to beautify the front and backyard. While the contracted workers were busy, Connie and I made a guest list that included family, friends, colleagues, and leaders in the community who had helped me cross the many dangerous and shaky bridges in my life. This was an opportunity to reciprocate some of the kind invitations we had received through the years. Once the above tasks were completed, we met with the caterers and selected the menu.

While all of this was happening, Connie met with a very creative, artistic colleague, and they came up with an unusual design for my invitations. The design was a trifold invitation with a pebbled surface in the color black, with a black and gold ribbon (Alpha Phi Alpha colors) surrounding the invitation. The invitation featured a colorful picture of a frog perched on a round disk. The frog held a banner that read, "Look Who's Turning 90." To open the invitation, one slid the ribbon attached to the frog up or down.

Why was a frog chosen? Well, frogs have always fascinated me, even though they are considered to be bad luck or bad omens in some cultures. While growing up in Farmville, they seemed magical and provided simple joys for me and my friends. My intellectual interests as a young, black boy turned more serious when I entered high school. I recall with fondness my first male teacher who happened to be the school principal and was also a biologist who taught us to study organisms using the scientific method. That teacher catalyzed my boyhood fascination with frogs into serious study, which included regular dissections of them. Dissecting a frog was a new frontier, and I remember with clarity the complex biological systems revealed to me as we used scissors, scalpels, pins, and gloves to peek inside of the them. I believe these were pivotal moments. They sowed the seeds that eventually inspired me to be a biologist.

About 30 years ago, I decided to start collecting frogs for fun. Frogs have had a variety of roles in many cultures, often appearing in art, fairy tales, and fables. In some cultures, they have been considered symbols of fertility, and in other cultures that worshipped animals they were sacred creatures. My personal collection now includes more than 200 frogs from all over the world. Each frog in my collection is different and possesses a different persona. They are made from all kinds of materials: wood, ceramics, clay, metal, etc. I enjoy looking at them and wonder what the Creator wanted to convey to us when he or she made them. For me, admiring them is like going to the Museum of Modern Art (MOMA) and spending time in its galleries. To connect with an individual amphibian (a frog), one must really look, see, and study the uniqueness that each one possesses.

I am particularly proud of the frogs I collected in China on a cruise with Connie up the Yangtze River in China in the 1980s. While on board, I purchased a three-legged frog with a coin in his mouth. I researched the significance of the frog and discovered it was a fortune frog, which plays a prominent role in the ancient Chinese art of feng shui. It symbolizes wealth, health, and prosperity, and when placed in your home or business brings to it money, good fortune, and health. Fortune frogs have red-eyes and are most often depicted sitting upon a pile of gold coins or Chinese money. These money frogs symbolized for all of the guests at my party my wish that wealth and good health would come their way.

The day of the party, Saturday, May 27, 2017, finally arrived. It was a warm day with the temperature hovering near eighty degrees. The sun was brightly shining in a clear blue sky, and we could not have asked for a nicer day. The banquet facility was beautifully decorated in gold and black, and my guests signed in and received their table assignments from one of three hostesses. A beautiful frog sat on the sign-in table to greet each guest. They were then escorted to their tables as a professional string trio from Cohoes, NY, played music by Bach, Vivaldi, Haydn, Handel, Telemann, and others. Connie and I tried our very best to great each guest personally and to reunite with those whom we hadn't seen for a long time. Videographers and photographers were present and tried to capture as many pictures and scenes as they could before, during, and after the event. The tables were covered in cream-colored tablecloths with black and gold napkins alternating on each plate. Courteous waitstaff served our guests sushi, crab balls, crudité, and hot and cold hors d'oeuvres.

The ballroom was also filled with people from all walks of life including medical doctors, Ph.D.'s, attorneys, bankers, state senators, local and state officials, economists, engineers, clergy, and many other professionals. Guests traveled from as far away as Kenya, Nigeria, Japan, Bosnia, Florida, California, North Carolina, Virginia, and Maryland. The ballroom was also filled with a rainbow of races including Blacks, Whites, Asians, and Africans. The diversity in the room reflected cultural, ethnic, and religious differences but also demonstrated community and inclusiveness. It was like a mini-United Nations. Love was in abundance, and the atmosphere was one of unity, friendship, and peace.

Connie began the ceremony by saying that, "Twitty is a multifaceted personality full of energy, enthusiasm, and reverence for life. He is a man who has touched many lives through his strength of character, generosity, caring, compassion, and his unflinching dedication to doing and saying what he thinks is right for the welfare of mankind. Twitty has an abiding interest in people, no matter who they are or where they may have come from." Connie then shared with our guests that I have been the "prince in the journey of her life." I was so moved. I felt her love and the love of my family and friends throughout the afternoon.

I am deeply humbled that 200 guests came that day to share my 90th birthday with me. Attendees ranged from four-months-old to 95-years-of-age. A representative from Governor Andrew Cuomo's office presented me with a special proclamation, and Senator Hugh Farley, one of New York's finest State Senators, attended. He spoke about my commitment to educating Union College students and to performing community service. On a prior occasion, the senator presented me with a beautiful medallion that recognized my military service in the Korean Conflict. I fondly recall teaching his daughter when she attended Union College in the 70s.

Other esteemed guests who spoke at the party included my "adopted little brother" and best friend, Professor Carl George from Union College. He shared his fond memories of our more than 50-year friendship. Carl composed a poem entitled "Big Man from Farmville," which he shared with our guests. It was a very touching tribute that attested to our mutual admiration and brotherhood. President Emeritus Roger Hull of Union College also made uplifting remarks, and family members and friends shared fond memories. It was an overwhelmingly upbeat event filled with friends, fun, food, and frogs.

Dinner consisted of a choice of four entrees: baked chicken, braised short ribs, salmon, or vegetarian food. Soft music played while guests ate their dinners and quietly talked with each other. Following dinner, Connie and I cut the delicious cake that was decorated with frosted icons of my favorite things and served to all.

After my birthday celebration, Connie and I invited family and close friends back to our home. We had an elaborate set-up in our backyard with catered, scrumptious soul food. Guests had the option of eating outside or inside, and there was lively conversation everywhere. Old friends reconnected, and family members were able to talk about shared memories and family news. Some guests remained at our home and enjoyed good food and company until almost midnight. On Sunday morning, most of the guests headed back home, but some were able to join us for breakfast. Overall, my 90th birthday party was a fabulous celebration filled with love, admiration, and grace. I will never forget it, and will forever cherish all who came and contributed to its success.

PAYING BACK

My nine decades of life have been truly blessed: I have tried to express my gratitude though participation in the service activities of organizations with a strong mission of community outreach.

A few years after coming to Union College, two of my colleagues in the Biology Department invited me to join the Schenectady Torch Club. The club is international in scope, has semi-autonomous local clubs, and is open to recognized professionals. Those who join embrace the club's mission to promote discussion and debate about intellectual, cultural, civic, religious, scientific, economic, and political subjects.

When I joined, membership was restricted to men, but in 1973 our club began to admit women, too. My favorite presentations to the club were two: "Zoonosis Diseases of Animals Common to Man" and "HIV and AIDS." Torch Club meetings were an experience in continuing education. Discussions could become heated to the point at which members would leave the room. The candor, passion, and knowledge presented for or against various points of view were always enriching. By the end of each meeting, we hoped that we had fostered a more comprehensive perspective on the topic under discussion for the evening. Sadly, the polarization of our national politics during President Trump's tenure has been upsetting and contrary to the ideals fostered by Torch Club members. Today, I am the oldest member of the club who attends the monthly dinners and discussion. I also have fond recollections of serving as secretary, vice-president, and president of the Torch Club during the 1980s.

On another note, I was a founding member of the Beta Psi Chapter of the Sigma Pi Phi Fraternity in Albany, New York. The fraternity is the oldest Black Greek lettered organization in the United States. The organization is called the Boulé, which means "a council of noblemen." It was founded in 1904 because blacks were not offered participation in the professional and cultural associations organized by the white community.

I served as the Sire Archon (the president) of the chapter during its formative years in the 1990s. It was during my tenure as president that the Albany chapter's vision and future goals were established. Our major objective was to establish college scholarships for deserving students. Today, we have achieved our goal, and have established a foundation that awards scholarships for which the selection is highly competitive. Scholarships are awarded to individuals based on demonstrated academic ability and personal character. The Boulé also holds a summer picnic premier each year to honor our wives (the Archousa) and significant others. It is a wonderful opportunity to network and fellowship with other black professionals in the Capital District of Albany.

When I came to Schenectady and was looking for housing, I was told to stay off the Hill because of the area's problems with drugs and gun violence. The Carver Community Center is located on the Hill and was established to serve the community's youth and families. The center housed a branch of the Schenectady County library and made books, computers, and other resources available for after-school programs that provided a safer alternative for young people to gather in than the street.

There were 16 members on the board. Many were legacy members and served because they had connections to the Center's founders. Several positions on the board were held by members who resided outside the community but who had a strong commitment to improving opportunities for residents of the Hill. I was one such board member. Suggestions from members outside of the area were not readily received, however. There was a pervasive attitude often expressed by the so-called "inside members" that things were going to be done their way, and if you raised concerns or objections, it was the highway. There was much bickering about policies and the election of officers. This strife led to the resignation of eight of the outside members of the board. This was followed by a vote of no confidence in the Director of the Center. He was a competent administrator but was consumed by internal politics. He and other directors came and went, but problems continued to grow. Carver finally closed its doors in 2013 and remains closed today. It's been a true loss to people of color in Schenectady.

On another note, the needs of veterans who have sacrificed so much for their fellow countrymen are often forgotten in the rush of our everyday lives. One day, following our Methodist church service, a fellow member who knew that I had served in the Korean Conflict invited me to join the Clifton Park-Halfmoon Post #1498 of the Veterans of Foreign Wars. The post has approximately 200 names on the roster. Only 15 to 20 attended meetings, however. Three years after joining, I was elected as Post Commander. I proudly assumed the duties of post commander, feeling a patriotic duty to do what I could to serve my fellow veterans. I am strongly motivated to serve them because of my personal memories of friends and family who sacrificed their lives for our country.

The goal of the Post is assist veterans, their widows, and their families in times of need. We also actively promote patriotism in our schools, and read over 300 essays each fall from elementary school students who have written essays on topics related to patriotism. We also march in Clifton Park's annual 4th of July parade, and raise funds on Memorial Day and Veterans Day. The funds raised support monetary awards to students whose essays on patriotism are judged to be outstanding.

I recall one cold and blustery November of 2011 day sitting in front of a local store. I had a coffee can in one hand while I passed out commemorative red poppies with the other. I heard the sound the donations made as people dropped them into the can. It was so cold that my hands were freezing, and I was shaking, despite wearing a pair of long johns that day.

I was moved when a very kind lady came by and gave me gloves she had purchased for me from a store nearby. I thanked her, and she thanked me for my service to the country. On another day, a woman went to the coffee shop and brought me coffee. On the other hand, I was invisible to some as they passed me by. They looked straight ahead, and chose not to donate. They were the exception, however. Many who passed by donated and understood the sacrifices that their grandfathers, fathers, and children made to keep our country safe. I lost a nephew in World War II in the Pacific, and many friends and comrades in the Korean War. We should never forget their ultimate sacrifice and the sacrifices of untold others who served our country so valiantly.

HONOR FLIGHT

The Leatherstocking Honor Flight (LHF) is part of the National Honor Flight Network. It is committed to recognizing American Veterans for their sacrifices and achievements during WWII and the Korean War. In October of 2014, the LHF honored me and my fellow local veterans by flying us to visit the Washington, D.C., -based memorials to our wartime service. We boarded busses and were escorted to the Albany Airport by two State Troopers and 20 members of the Patriot Guard motorcyclists. At the airport, 200 people were waiting for us and greeted us with flags, banners, two choirs, and a band to give us a grand and rousing sendoff. What a surprise! It was a great feeling to be among other veterans. One of the veterans on the trip to D.C. was 100-years-old at the time. When we arrived at Baltimore-Washington International Airport, we were met for a second time with flags, banners, and wonderful, heartfelt appreciation for our service.

It is not every day that a person is greeted by a former veteran, war hero, leader of the U.S. Senate, and the 1996 candidate for President of the United States. When we arrived in Washington, D.C, we were greeted by just such a person: Senator Robert Dole, a true patriot. Students from many colleges and universities were there to greet and take pictures with us, too. We had the opportunity to visit the World War II Memorial, the Iwo Jima

Memorial, the Vietnam Memorial, the Lincoln Monument, and the Korean War Memorial. When we arrived at it, I was overcome with emotion. Thoughts of so many of the buddies I lost in it flooded back. I spent an hour there in deep thought and remembrance. Upon close examination of the names engraved on the memorial, I could see soldiers that represented many ethnic groups: Blacks, Caucasians, Latinos, and Asians. President Harry Truman integrated the U.S. Army in 1948.

After our stops at the various memorials, we travelled to Arlington Cemetery to see the changing of the guards at the Tomb of the Unknown Soldiers. It was very impressive. There were approximately 200 people there, yet you could hear a pin drop. Taps were sounded, and there was not a dry eye in the crowd. I thought to myself in that hushed and reverent crowd that many of those gathered there that day had been connected in various ways to soldiers who sacrificed their lives so that America could be free.

On the plane ride home, a man who was playing the role of "summer" Santa Claus came with a package of mail for each of us. The mail was the work of elementary school students and teachers, and contained American flags and images of bald eagles and other patriotic icons. The distribution of the mail was reminiscent of roll call in the Army. One of my brother veterans said it was one of the best days in his life. It was exciting, moving, and sobering.

The LHF was truly uplifting for me. I was so touched that caring citizens would do so much to honor the past service rendered by this man of color (me) to his country. It contrasted deeply with the feelings of negativity, hostility, discrimination, and prejudice I had experienced throughout my life.

FACES AND PLACES

CONNIE

My wife is a superlative woman. She deserves a diamond tiara. She is an outstanding wife, mother, and pediatrician. Some of her patients go back three generations. A wall in our home is covered with accolades for her kind and generous professional service and her contributions to the Capital District: she has earned a "Best Doctor in the Capital District" award for many years. She's a liturgist and communion steward at our church and volunteers in other capacities when needed. In 2017, the Town of Clifton Park even awarded her a "Key to the Town" for her community service. Her passion for delivering old time true medical care is unwavering, and she is a true pioneer. In fact, she was the only black female among ten women in her 150-student medical school Class of 1960 at Downstate Medical Center, in Brooklyn, New York. During the late 50s and early 60s, all women who wanted to pursue careers in medicine had a hard time, but the challenges and obstacles for black women were even greater.

When her mother and father became elderly and were unable to take care of themselves, she never thought of placing them in a nursing home. They came to live with us. Our children were in elementary school at the time, but she went to her office each day, cooked, got the children ready for school, and took care of her parents. I recall that even though she didn't approve, she indulged her father with a daily glass of liquor. It turned out that he lived to be 95. Just like my father, Connie and I always placed a high value on the education of our children. We fostered in our two children, Scott and Auria, a love of learning, and a love of travel: When they were young, we took them to Canada, Mexico, Puerto Rico, Colombia, and Jamaica. Now, they are world travelers in their own right.

Connie always graciously opened our home to my college students. I recall that at least once each term in the 60s and 70s she would prepare dinner for them. She would create an intimate and personal setting so that students could unwind and talk about things unrelated to school. These gatherings were fun for Connie and me because they gave us the opportunity to connect with students outside the confines of the classroom environment. As a result, our family developed friendships with former students' families from all over the world.

The following vignettes represent my personal recollections of some (but nowhere near all) of our extended family members who made significant impressions on my life. Many were able to attend my ninetieth birthday celebration.

SEYMOUR

Sy, as we affectionately call him, has been our friend, counselor, and advisor since 1965. He practiced law in Manhattan before retiring to Boca Raton, Florida. After our first meeting, he took a "liking to us," and our friendship flourished and grew ever closer over the years. He was a brilliant lawyer, avid reader, and prolific writer. We have been included in his weddings, funerals, and family occasions. He attended both Scott and Auria's graduations from Princeton, and we visited him at his home in Boca Raton,

Florida, in January of 2017. We spent two days talking about our families' peaks and valleys, joys and sorrows.

I was delighted he could join our family and friends to celebrate my 90th birthday. At the celebration, he said, "I never thought I would meet a black family and form such a bond." At 95, Sy cut a sharp figure sporting a distinctive beard and moustache. His mind remains sharp. The physical ailments that come with advanced age have not diminished his ability to have fun. What a joy it was to have him attend my birthday celebration.

Fast forward 15 months. Sy called us on August 1, 2018, and told us he was in hospice. He thanked us for our friendship and told us how much he loved us. He was part of our family, and we will always remember his kind spirit and love for humankind. He passed on August 19, 2018. Gone but not forgotten. I miss him dearly.

HAMAKI

I was shocked when Hamaki Hara emailed me and said that she and her son Taketoshi would be coming from Nagoya, Japan, to attend my 90th birthday celebration. Hamaki was a 13-year-old AFS student whom we had hosted for a summer more than 30 years ago. While she was here, she taught us about Japanese culture, cooking, eating, manners, and etiquette, and we taught her about the American versions of the same. Furthermore, we took her to many museums, parks, and concerts at the Saratoga Performing Arts Center where she heard the Philadelphia Orchestra and saw the New York City ballet.

Our friends and neighbors, Dan and Rosemarie Johnson, had two daughters, Mitzi and Carrie, around the same age as Hamaki. Coincidentally, they also hosted an AFS student that summer named Kristien, who was from Belgium. It was a summer of fun, festivities, and frolic but for one incident that almost ended in tragedy. One Sunday afternoon, the Johnsons invited our family and a few other teenagers to take a ride on their boat in Lake George. Everyone was excited about the trip, donned their bathing suits, and lathered on suntan lotion for the occasion. When we arrived at Lake George, we boarded the boat, Dan started the motor, and after about 30 minutes found an area of the lake that was very calm. He stopped the boat and allowed everyone who wanted to swim to jump in the lake. One by one, like excited green bull frogs, the children jumped in. However, when Hamaki jumped in no one knew she couldn't swim. She immediately began to have trouble treading water, so Dan threw her a life preserver and rescued her. For a few moments, it was a scary situation that we all still remember to this day.

Fast forward about 20 years. On our way back from one of our trips to China in the 1990s, she and her family hosted us at a hotel for about a week. We met many members of her immediate and extended family, and they took us to visit Kyoto, Nara, and other famous places. We were quite lucky because we arrived at the peak of the cherry blossom season, and Nagoya and its countryside were regaled with the most beautiful cherry blossoms imaginable.

Eight years ago, when Taketoshi was 12, Hamaki and her family came to visit us. They spent a week with us and then went to New York City to do some sightseeing. Our cousin, Winnette, who lives in Manhattan, hosted them for a few days and took them to see many attractions. They returned home saturated with fond memories.

Today, our families communicate regularly by email and FaceTime. In fact, when Connie sent out the "Save the Date" cards in February of 2017 for my 90th birthday celebration, Hamaki was the first to call and say that she and her son would be attending. They arrived on May 24, and left on May 29, but played an important role in making my birthday celebration a tremendous success. The mascots of the party were frogs, and on the morning of the party, Connie and her friends had placed on each table an upright green frog with a crown on it. The night before the party, Hamaki and Taketoshi had hand-made 200 origami frogs out of bright-colored paper. (Origami is the Japanese art of making objects out of paper.) These frogs could even "hop" on flat surfaces if we pressed down on their rear ends! Hamaki and Taketoshi tried to teach me how to make origami frogs, but needless to say, I am still practicing this art. Our guests loved them, however, and throughout the party talked about how lovely they were.

On another note, Hamaki's father is a beekeeper, and up until a few years ago, she helped him periodically keep them. One day while changing her shoes she was stung by a bee, had an allergic reaction, and had to be hospitalized. Now, she stays away from bees. Her son Taketoshi is studying civil engineering at college, and one day hopes to design bridges. We enjoyed their visit for my 90th birthday party, and we plan to keep in touch with them well into the future.

PATTI

When Connie's father came to live with us, we hired a caregiver to assist with his care when we were at work. That caregiver was Patti. Patti was a 5' 5" platinum blonde who weighed about 140 lbs. She gave him lunch and made sure he took his medicine. Patti's personal life was not always an easy one. Her husband was an alcoholic, and she had two sons living with them that had difficulty finding employment. We tried to support her whenever we could. One day, I overheard Patti speaking on the phone. Someone wanted to speak to my wife. She replied, "My madam is not home, call back later." That was a phrase I heard many years ago in the South, when black women worked for "Miss Ann." Patti got joy out of simple things. I recall her love for her two little Yorkies, and the fun she had playing bingo. When she passed, I helped arrange and pay for most of her funeral. I miss my friend.

MIKE

For his freshman year some 30 years ago, Mike was hired to be my grant-in-aid student (laboratory assistant) at the college. He made sure the animals were cared for and the animal room was clean. He also assisted me in the preparation of teaching materials used in the laboratory. In class, we did many hands on mini-experiments with live animals, and he learned many valuable laboratory procedures. He was astonished to find out the vital role laboratory animals played in medical research.

Mike enrolled in several of my courses, and was particularly interested in the protocols that involved surgery. He completed an independent research project with me and graduated with honors. Today, he is a surgeon and happily married with three beautiful children. He and his family never fail to visit us during the holiday season. My wife always prepares broccoli especially for him. Years ago, he didn't like it, but now he does!

JOY CABARRUS SPEAKES

Joy Cabarrus Speakes was a freshman at Moton H.S. in 1951 when I taught there. We did not know each other at the time, but both of us were witness to the tar paper shacks and wooden stoves in our dilapidated school. During 1951-1964, the years of turmoil and strife, a cross was burned on the grounds of our school. Despite this and other attempts to intimidate and frighten the black community, we were determined to fight for an end to separate and unequal schools in PEC. The fire of our defiance was lit and was not going to be extinguished until we had won the battle.

I first met Joy in August 2016 when I was visiting the Moton Museum. She invited me and my family to a Family Challenge meeting to discuss scholarships for children whose ancestors were denied an education during the closing of schools in PEC from 1959-1964. Many of my relatives were among this group. Her presentation was very compelling, and I pledged a donation on the spot. I did this because she and many of my colleagues and friends risked their lives fighting for equal educational opportunity and the desegregation of schools. The sizeable monetary pledge that I made to the fund was the least I could do. Joy serves on the Moton Museum Council and is the chair of development for the Moton Museum. She works tirelessly to make the museum the very best it can be.

I volunteered to help her solicit funds for the museum-sponsored scholarships, and so far, the fund has received donations from 30 of my friends and co-workers. She has also been a catalyst for keeping the link between Longwood College and the Moton Museum very strong. I was honored when she decided to attend my 90th birthday celebration. There, Mrs. Speakes gave a moving account of the history of the museum, and made a compelling case for donations to the Museum and its scholarship fund.

SADE AND AYO

My family adopted Queenie Sawyer (Sade) around 1975. At that time, faculty at Union volunteered to be mentors and advisors for incoming freshmen, and we were fortunate to be paired with her, a young lady from Lagos, Nigeria. I took her home to meet my family, and she soon became a member.

Because I was on campus daily, I kept an eye on her. Furthermore, my wife included her in our family and holiday gatherings, and taught her about American culture. She often visited our home because she was more than 3000 miles away from her family. It must have been difficult for her to be 3,000 miles away from family, loved ones, and friends—What a culture shock! Towards the end of her undergraduate years at Union, she met her husband, Ayo Coker, a physicist at the State University of New York—Albany, and subsequently they were married in Union College's chapel. Auria was six-years-old then, and was the flower girl at their wedding.

A few years later, they had a son, Deji. He was nine-months-old when, sadly, Queenie lost her mother. She and Ayo had to return to Africa to make funeral arrangements, and it was difficult for them to take the baby with them, so they left their baby with us. He was a strong, muscular bundle of joy. He never lacked attention from us, but I recall that he wasn't a good sleeper. After the funeral, Sade and Ayo were told that they could not leave Lagos due to a technical issue with Sade's passport. After marriage, her name changed from Sawyer to Coker, and that created the problem. They were detained for around four weeks until they could get clearance to leave from the Nigerian Immigration Department. It wasn't easy for them: They had to pull as many strings as possible to leave.

Finally, they returned home and found that Deji was well cared for. As he grew up, I taught him how to drive. Deji went on to earn his under-graduate degree at SUNY and his Ph.D. from Texas A&M University. He married a young Nigerian woman named Yette, and invited us to attend and participate in their weekend wedding in London. It was a dual cere-mony wedding: The first day was a traditional African wedding service followed by a dinner. The second day was a Christian wedding service held in a huge Anglican church followed by a beautiful evening reception. Many ladies wore colorful Nigerian dresses with wraps on their heads. The men had on their finest formal suits, and everyone had a great time. Today, Deji and his family live in London. Now, we have a loving family with three grandchildren: Steven, from Scott and Jessica, and two from Deji and Yette.

REUBEN AND ADDIE

In August 1964, we arrived in Mexico City after a six-week cross country journey. We stayed in a hotel while looking for an apartment. While in Mexico, I had an experience that is etched in my memory. There was a doorway connecting our dining room to our bedroom. I awoke one night to see my deceased father standing in the doorway. He was dressed in a white shirt with dark trousers. I could have touched him he was so real. He did not speak—he just stood there, staring at us. All these years later, his visit remains a vivid and clear memory. I shook Connie to wake her. I told her we had a visitor. In the time it took for me to rouse Connie from her sleep, he was gone. How strange! He has not been back since. Was he trying to tell me something? I don't know.

Our apartment was on the second floor, and our neighbors that lived across the hall were Reuben, Addie, and their family. He was an accountant, and she a housewife. They had a maid, Angela, who took care of the cleaning for them. We also were able to employ Angela. She had two sons, Tonio and Enrique, who were four- and six-years-old. Angela and her sons lived on the top floor of the apartment complex where most of the maids and their families dwelled. Angela became a member of our family and was very kind to us. She had native Indian heritage, and we got along well with her and her family. Angela talked to us in Spanish, and her boys learned some English from us. We had great conversations.

Addie knew that I was a parasitologist and was doing a post-doctoral fellowship at the National Medical School. I told her I was working on intestinal parasites and other tropical diseases. She knew that I was not only concerned about "gusanos," roundworms, but also about harmful amoebas that can invade the body and do damage to the liver, intestines, and other organs. One day, Addie told me, "Me duele mi estomago." Her stomach hurt because she was suffering from a chronic amoebic infection that flared up and was painful that day. Unfortunately, I was not able to treat her but told her to visit the doctor as soon as possible.

Connie and I took many precautions to keep healthy during our stay in Mexico. One was always using bottled or boiled water because parasitic diseases can be transmitted by contaminated food and water. Another was washing all of our vegetables and fruit with non-contaminated water containing mild detergent. We were always careful not to eat anything sold by vendors on the streets.

At Christmas, we decided to have a Christmas party for the less privileged children in the apartment complex. Six-year-old Patrice lived on the first floor, and would greet us with her big smile and dark penetrating eyes. Her parents allowed us to have the party in their apartment. Ten boys and girls were invited. We had a Christmas tree with all the holiday trimmings, and had purchased small gifts for everyone. They sang carols in Spanish, and we taught them "Jingle Bells" in English. What a festive occasion! The children screamed with delight, and we were overjoyed to bring some cheer to them. A good time was had by all.

Our apartment was like a hotel, and we had a waiting list for visitors. Connie's mother came, as did other friends and relatives. We warned my cousin and her family from California to be careful with food, particularly lettuce, water, and anything from street vendors, but our advice was not always heeded. One of my cousins came to visit us, took a trip to Acapulco, and when she returned from her trip, made a beeline for the toilet. (Montezuma's Revenge had gotten a hold of her, too!)

When we were ready to leave, Angela came to our apartment to say goodbye, sobbing. I gave her a hug and a sheet of paper with our address. I asked her to write to us and keep in touch. She stopped crying, looked at us, and handed the pencil back to me and said, "No escribe, Senor." We were surprised that our dear friend had not had the opportunity to obtain a formal education. It was sad that such an intelligent person had not been taught to read and write. We have missed her a lot over the years.

BAC

About 25 years ago, Bac Nguyen applied for a grant-in-aid position in the biology department at Union College. After the interview, I knew I was going to hire him. He told me about growing up in Vietnam and what he had to do to come to the U.S. as a refugee. He grew up in a foster home in New York along with his two brothers and other foster children. He attended Suffern High School and then enrolled at Union college where he met his future wife, Linh. A few days after the interview, I let him know he had been accepted. At the time, I was chairperson of the biology department.

Bac took two of my courses and learned a tremendous amount of practical laboratory techniques. He earned an A, then asked to do research with me. I eagerly added him to my list of research students. He worked on the *in vitro* cultivation of *Pneumocystis carinii*, the organism that was identified in 1980 as being heavily involved with AIDS patients. At the time, it was thought that leaning more about *P. carinii* would help to alleviate some of the opportunistic infections found in patients with AIDS. Bac used a fluorescent whitener and bright dye to aid in the visualization of *P. carinii* in culture. His work was approved by two other professors in the department, and he graduated with honors. At Union, he was a member of Unitas and was elected to Phi Beta Kappa. After graduating from Union with honors, he attended Dartmouth Medical School and Brown University School of Medicine. Recently, he has been named to the American Health Council Physician's Board. What an honor! We attended his graduation and his wedding. He and his family attended my 90th birthday celebration, and we consider them part of our family, too.

ESTELLE

Estelle was one of the hundred women in Union's first coed class. I remember her as a petite young lady with an overwhelming amount of energy and intelligence. She graduated in the Class of 1974, and I have followed her from her freshman year in college until now. She flew up from Washington, D.C., just to celebrate my birthday and returned the same day.

While at Union, I watched her as a student and was her unofficial advisor in her pre-medical courses. She was bright, inquisitive, and determined to study medicine. As with all biology students, each one was special to me. I was on her premedical committee and found that she had been actively engaged in volunteering her time and talent to others. She was a member of the Union College Drama Club and the Black Student Alliance, and had worked with many underprivileged residents of Hamilton Hill. She always studied hard, and had a pleasing personality and disposition. Her desire to help others manifests itself today.

After graduating from Georgetown Medical School, she became Associate Professor of Radiology at Howard University in Washington, D.C., served as a medical officer with the U.S. Public Health Service, and worked in women's health care. I recommended her for a seat on the Union Board of Trustees, and she was selected enthusiastically, having served several terms now. The college has been one of the premier recipients of her time, talent, and resources. She and her brothers Gerald and Lawrence set up the Cooke Family Scholarship in 1977.

My wife and I consider her our daughter, and when I was a Visiting Professor of Biology at Marymount University, in Arlington, Virginia, she arranged to have us be the guests of honor at her home in northwest Washington, D.C. It was a gala affair.

Estelle's oldest daughter also attended Union. She was not a biology major, and unfortunately, I did not see her as often as I did her mother. When she graduated, Connie and I hosted a graduation party at our home, and invited Estelle's friends, family, and Union faculty to the event. Recently, we were honored to attend her oldest daughter's wedding held at the exclusive

Army and Navy Club in Arlington, Virginia, overlooking the Capitol.

She has been honored by so many organizations, foundations, clubs, and communities. She is one who cares, shares, and never forgets the bridges that brought her across.

BEN

In the summer of 2017, when I answered the telephone, I was pleased to know that it was Dr. Benjamin Rubin, Class of 1975, asking me if he could stop by with his wife and son. "Of course," I said. It is always a pleasure to welcome a former student into your home. They came, and we spent hours talking about the past. Ben is an orthodox Jew. During our conversation, he recalled the unwelcome reception he received from some students when he was an undergraduate at Union. At that time, he wore a yarmulke and owned a pet schnauzer that he often walked around campus with. He was often taunted with anti-Semitic remarks and gestures, however, and often felt like an outsider in the predominantly white Anglo-Saxon protestant world of Union College.

On a positive note, he also recounted how he was responsible for the establishment of a kosher kitchen at Union, and was a leader on campus. Moreover, I was his research advisor and mentored his biology project. I'm proud to say that he worked hard, was an excellent student, and graduated with honors in the department. His mother, Lucille, was a very successful ophthalmologist who was highly respected in both the U.S. and in Europe.

One day, she sat in on one of my classes during a visit to campus. That day, my lecture focused on a filarial worm disease that can lead to blindness. A few days later, she went home and sent me some very valuable Kodachrome slides of parasitic diseases of the eye. They were valuable teaching tools that enhanced my presentations. After her visit, I got to know his family very well, and we became friends.

Later that year, I was a visiting professor at Marymount University in Arlington, Virginia, and Ben was doing research at the National Institutes of Health (NIH). It was then that I learned that his mother relocated from New York to Washington because she had cancer. I was able to visit her several times in the hospital. She kept her beautiful outlook on life and was very upbeat, but she passed away a few months later.

I have kept in touch with Ben and his family, and was as proud as a peacock when he told me he was an ophthalmologist, Rabbi, and inventor with many papers in refereed journals. He offered to come back to Union and give a talk about his success. Our visit ended with a promise to keep in touch. Ben was the kind of student that always gave 100% of his effort, and was an inspiration to others. It is always gratifying to have former students like Ben take the time to visit me and reminisce about the past.

LYDIA

I was invited to be the Professor-in-Residence in Costa Rica during the winter term of 1992. It was a ten-week term abroad in environmental studies, political science, and Spanish. I arrived a week ahead of the students to meet with the professors, and we talked about the syllabi, curriculum, and logistics of the program. A few days later, I found an apartment that required me to walk six blocks to take a bus to the school.

At the end of the week, the group arrived: seven girls and four boys. They were assigned to host families with whom they resided. My task was to contribute to the environmental studies portion of the curriculum, to make sure that they went to classes and completed their homework, and to keep them safe. Prior to leaving the U.S., I had sent to Costa Rica a box of books and reference guides for them, as well.

After a few weeks of classes, I began to get complaints from host families about our students' behavior. The families were very strict and expected them to come home before midnight. Many of the girls didn't obey the rules and had to be changed to other families. Some students complained to me about roosters crowing and awakening them at 5:00 a.m. What could I do? Nothing.

Some of the girls expected it would be a home-away-from-home and a ten-week vacation. Four of the girls stayed together most the time, and didn't have to worry about money. Three were not well off and had to monitor their spending money. These two groups of girls didn't associate much with each other.

One day, a young student named Lydia asked me at the end of January if she could be absent from classes from Wednesday until the following Monday. I asked her why.

She replied, "My cousin is coming up from Brazil, and I need time to show her around."

I said, "No, you don't have my permission to miss class, because your grades will be affected."

When I returned to campus at the end of the term in March, the director of Union College Terms Abroad called me into his office. I debriefed him about what went on during the courses.

He said, " Twitty, I know you don't know this."

I said, "Know what?'"

He replied, "I was in Seville, Spain, at the end of January. Guess who I saw coming down the street in Seville?"

"Who?"

He replied, "I was sitting at an outdoor café, and Lydia (the student who was on the term abroad in Costa Rica), was walking down the street with her boyfriend. He was also on a term abroad from another college and studying in Spain at the time. She had skipped classes in Costa Rica to fly to Spain to see her boyfriend."

I was so flabbergasted that all I could say was "Well!"

VERA

When my family moved from Five Forks to Farmville, our next-door neighbor was Mrs. Womack. She owned her home but lived in New Jersey for most of the year (she vacationed for three weeks at her home in Farmville). Often, she spoke about her cataracts and how hard it was for her to see things. At the time, I had no idea about cataracts. I now do because I have had surgery to remove them from both of my eyes. I asked my doctor, "What causes cataracts?" and he replied, "Old age." But, I recall Mrs. Womack sitting on her porch in her rocking chair saying that the cause of cataracts was "Memories, memories, sweet memories."

When I was in the seventh grade, a black southern gentleman named Paige and his wife, Vera, rented Mrs. Womack's house. Paige owned a cleaning and pressing shop, and Vera was his housewife. He was exceedingly jealous, so I was hired to stay with his wife until he came home in the evening. I took my books over and studied at Ms. Womack's house until he came home. Shockingly, one night, she showed me a pistol. I had never seen one before. At the time, World War II was in progress, and Camp Pickett, an Army base, was in Blackstone, Virginia, 20 miles away. Many of the women in Farmville volunteered to visit the camp on weekends, and Vera was one of them. Two years later, Page and Vera moved to the outskirts of town into a brick home. One day, she shot Paige in a domestic dispute. She used the gun that she had shown me a few years before. She was charged with murder and sentenced to life in prison. I was shocked that I had known such a woman.

CLOSING THOUGHTS

Along my life's journey, many things have happened to me. And, I believe that my life has been guided by the Creator. I believe that I have been blessed with a divine (not man-made) GPS that has helped me find my way through the trials, tribulations, and vicissitudes of life.

When I was a little boy, I never thought that I would ever get out of PEC, but I managed not only to do so but to see the world. Even though I carry clouds and shadows with me every day, I am a resilient person who is able to deal with what life sends my way. I have found that most insults and derogatory words directed towards me have come from ignorant people. They have been taught how to hate: they have not learned the skills that foster communication, understanding, and acceptance of individuals with different ethnic backgrounds or religions from their own. That is why I am devoted to Unitas, which tries to break down ignorance and xenophobia by promoting diversity and community. Every day when I wake up, I put on my "protective armor" and am ready for any encounter. I know that Caucasian people have privileges only because of the color of their skin.

When I meet negative situations and people, I also remember Psalms 27:1: "The LORD is my light and my salvation; whom shall I fear? The LORD is the strength of my life; of whom shall I be afraid?" [3]

I frequently turn to Scripture to guide, fortify, and strength me to "Dance with the Devil" or to summon the better angels in me and in all of us.

The journey I have recounted was not written over the course of a few days or weeks. It is the product of spurts of recollection and inspiration. I started 20 years ago, and thought that I would have nothing to say. When I began to put pen to paper, my mind vault opened like a water spigot. Most of my thoughts came to me around 4:00 a.m., so I regularly wrote and revised the text early in the morning. As with all autobiographies, much has been left out, including some of the more painful memories. Like everyone who lives a rich and productive life, there were high mountaintops and low valleys: disputes with family, town officials, academic colleagues, neighbors, and church and club members. Whenever attacked or mistreated, however, I have tried my best (not always perfectly) to remain calm, realizing people can act poorly out of ignorance. I have tried to put them on my prayer list and move forward. Prayer is, I believe, a powerful agent for change.

I am a son of Prince Edward County, a place full of fond memories of family and friends. A place whose people made history and a place that is part of my very soul. A place where my black brothers and sisters struggled courageously to fight the Jim Crow south. A place that's exemplary of America's struggle to make America a welcoming place for all.

Today, in Prince Edward County, the schools are integrated, and black professors and students can be found at Longwood University and Hampden Sydney College in Farmville. There are employees with good paying jobs, and a landmark Civil Rights Museum right in town. It is a place where Megan L. Clark, a black woman, serves as the current Commonwealth Attorney of Farmville. She was appointed in 2015. Yes, positive changes have

---

[3] The King James Study Bible: King James Version. London: Cambridge U, 1769.
Print; "King James Bible." King James Bible Online. N.p., 2017.

been made, but citizens must continue to build bridges of understanding that can lead to peace and harmony for all. In April of 2017, the entire Town of Farmville came together to honor Barbara Rose Johns by renaming the Farmville-Prince Edward County Library in her honor.

I have been truly blessed to have had so many positive friends, colleagues, and family members who have been mentors and supporters of me on my pilgrimage. I don't envy anyone, and I respect the achievements of others. I have worked my fingers to the bone since I was fourteen-years-old, and have no sleepless nights of guilt or regret about cheating my way in life or in my career.

When I am asked, "Where are you from?" it surprises me that so many people have never heard of Prince Edward County or its significance in the *Brown v Board of Education* Supreme Court ruling. And, like all of us, sometimes I wonder, "Why I am here? Do I have a special mission and purpose in life? I don't often have an answer, but feel like I am an oracle committed to spreading the truth about the history of Prince Edward County and its segregated past. My perspective on life was formed from having been born and raised there.

And, as I close this memoir, how do I want to be remembered? That's up to the people who knew me. However, I can say that in Sunday School and church, I was taught about "Standing the test in judgment." My father taught me that I am the master of my fate and the captain of my soul, so when I come to the end of my journey, I hope God will understand what I did in this life, and say, "Well done, my good and faithful servant!"

Ha! Ha! Now, that I am on "Highway 92," I have decided to stop counting the years, and I shall remain 90 forever with the time I have left.

EPILOGUE

On July 1, 2018, the term of Union College's 19th president began. David R. Harris, Ph.D., is a distinguished and innovative teacher, scholar, and administrator. Since Union's founding in 1795, there has never been an African-American chosen to lead the College. His presidency marks a new and exciting epoch in Union's history. When I joined Union's faculty more than 50 years ago, I would never have imagined such an appointment as a possibility. During my time at Union, I have seen many things change: Barriers were erected, but they have also been taken down. I am delighted to celebrate his appointment and wish him well in all of his endeavors.

At this divided and fractious time in our country's history, his presidency at Union is a strong symbol of the national inclusiveness we all should strive to achieve in America. I have positive hope for the future of Union and for the future of America.

Sincerely yours,

Twitty J. Styles, Ph.D.

The author's father, Peter Styles, was born in 1892. Pa, as he was called by Twitty and his siblings, was a skilled electrician and linesman employed by the Virginia Electric Power Company (VEPCO). He was frugal, industrious, fond of learning, and kind with unfailing good manners. Peter moved his family from Five Forks to Farmville because he realized the school system was not conducive to educating his family. Twitty's pursuit of advanced graduate degrees and a career in academia is, in no small part, a reflection of Peter's insight that a good education was necessary for success.

The author at 14 at Chappell's Fountain and Bookstore in downtown Farmville, Virginia. He worked there before school started in the morning, afternoons, and all-day Saturday. Twitty scrubbed floors, stocked shelves and made sandwiches and drinks for the "movers and shakers" of Farmville. Money earned was saved for college. He still recalls the sting of working hard but never being recognized as a person. He was the nice, invisible black boy.

Twitty with his M1 rifle standing proud and tall. He posed for this photo after completing his basic training at Fort Jackson, South Carolina. The young soldier returned to base after a two week leave to learn that his battalion was shipping off to Korea. His ship sailed during the winter of 1950.

Twitty enjoying R & R leave away from his military duties at the 406th Medical General Laboratory, 1951, near Mt. Fuji, Tokyo, Japan.

U.S. military, civilian and Japanese staff at the 406th Medical General Laboratory in Tokyo, Japan, 1952. It was at this laboratory that the author was introduced to medical protozoology and parasitology. This experience led to his pursuit of a Ph.D. in these fields and a career in academia.

Corporal Twitty J. Styles mustered out of the recently integrated U.S. Army in 1952 at age 25. He sent this picture taken in Tokyo, Japan, to his family in segregated Farmville, VA. He planned to pursue post-graduate studies in New York City using the education benefit of the G.I. Bill.

The former Robert Russa Moton High School in Farmville, VA, is a national historic landmark and home to the Robert Russa Moton Museum. The site commemorates the historic student-led civil rights walkout that ultimately led to court-ordered school desegregation. Originally built to house 140 students, the segregated school could not accommodate the more than 450 students that actually attended. Inadequate "temporary" tar paper shack style classrooms (insert) were built by the school board. The author was a student at R.R. Moton high school for four years. After completing college, he returned to Moton as a biology teacher.

The author's brothers and sisters. Seated, left to right, Luther, Florence, Leora and Arsenia. Standing, left to right, Calvin, Lloyd, Lawrence and Twitty.

Mexico Field Trip. In 1965, Twitty traveled to Mexico as a post-doctoral fellow sponsored by the U.S. Public Health Service. He is shown above, fourth from left with fellow scientists as they prepare to go on a scientific field trip. They were studying <u>onchocerciasis</u> (also known as river blindness). It is a filarial disease caused by a worm, <u>Onchocerca volvulus</u>. Infection can result in blindness.

This photo was taken in 1965 at a field research station in the Mexican jungle. Shown, left to right, Jorge Tay, Newton King, the author and Edward Berg.

Union College Biology Faculty posing by a large gingko tree in Jackson's Garden, Union College, late fall, 1966. Bottom, left to right, Raymond Rappaport, Francis Lambert, Leonard Clark (Department Chair), the author's wife, Constance Glasgow, Henry Butzel, the author, and Hans Rosenthal. Top, left to right, Melvin Fine and James Barlow.

A day of smiles, top hats, cravats and formal attire: Twitty and his close friend and colleague Carl J. George smile at their 1997 joint retirement celebration. They continue their service to the college community as professors 'emeriti. Carl and Twitty have been called by friends, "brothers from another mother."

In 1997, Twitty Styles, Connie Styles, Gail George and Carl George joined forces to establish Unitas at Union College. They recognized that we are all enriched when a community acts to foster, in the broadest sense, unity, diversity and multiculturalism. In a society that is polarized, the need to foster unity and community remains an urgent task.

Twitty, with his wife, Connie, and friends Wim and Anny Platteborze, in front of the restored Leuven University Library. Originally built in 1425, it was twice destroyed by invading German troops: first in 1915 and again in 1940. After WWI and WWII, books and funds were donated by allied and neutral countries for its restoration. Contributions from Union College are commemorated by an engraved stone plaque (insert, lower right).

Senator Bob Dole with Twitty (rear) and fellow veterans. They were flown to Washington, D.C., to honor their service and allow them to visit their memorials and reflect. It was a Leatherstocking Honor Flight that was offered to WWII and Korean War veterans living in the Capital District area of NY.

The author and his wife, Constance Glasgow, MD, have been married for 55 years. They raised their two children, Scott and Auria, in Clifton Park, NY, where Connie was the first pediatrician to practice in the community. She continues to serve the community. The Styles have a grandson, Steven.

Hamaki Hara and her son Taketoshi traveled 6,700 miles from Nagoya, Japan, to celebrate the author's 90th birthday. Top, left to right, Taketoshi, Hamaki, the author's daughter, Auria, and Twitty. Below, the author's son Scott with Taketoshi.

Twitty's family and friends gathered to celebrate his 90th birthday. They recalled with him the people and places and events that touched him along his life journey. Above is a photo of the frog-themed cake they shared with him.